GREAT MOVIE SPECTACULARS

Other books by the author:

GREAT MOVIE SPECTACULARS

by Edward Edelson

Doubleday & Company, Inc., Garden City, New York

LIBRARY OF CONGRESS CATALOGING IN PUBLICATION DATA

EDELSON, EDWARD, 1932–

GREAT MOVIE SPECTACULARS.

INCLUDES INDEX.

SUMMARY: TRACES THE HISTORY AND DISCUSSES THE APPEAL
OF THE FILM EPIC FROM THE EARLY 1900s TO THE PRESENT DAY.

1. MOVING-PICTURES—HISTORY—JUVENILE LITERATURE.
[1. MOTION PICTURES—HISTORY]   I. TITLE.

PN1994.5.E3   791.43'09

ISBN 0-385-11179-7 TRADE

    0-385-11180-0 PREBOUND

LIBRARY OF CONGRESS CATALOG CARD NUMBER 76–56

Contents

GREAT MOVIE SPECTACULARS

Grandeur and Glory, Thrills and Vistas

THE SCENE IS ANCIENT ROME; the year is 45 B.C. Cleopatra, queen of Egypt, is sailing up the Tiber in her royal barge for a triumphant entrance. The barge sweeps on majestically, its hundreds of oars perfectly synchronized, its purple sails billowing, with handmaidens strewing the water with coins and flowers. . . .

The scene is Pearl Harbor; the date is December 7, 1941. The Japanese have launched a sneak attack, and their aircraft are wreaking havoc on Battleship Row. Hardly affected by the Americans' feeble efforts at defense, the Japanese bomb and strafe the harbor, and the great American battleships, backbone of the fleet, are ripped apart by explosions. . . .

The scene is Balaklava in the Crimea; the year is 1854. The British are fighting the Russians, and through some blunder, a small brigade of lightly armed cavalry has been ordered to make a suicidal attack on a strong Russian position. As guns to the right and left of them volley and thunder, into the valley of death charge the gallant six hundred. . . .

The scene is Babylon in far ancient times. The splendid city is being attacked by the army of Cyrus the Persian, and the fabled walls of Babylon are crowded with thousands of warriors who try to fight off the assault of the huge war machines of the Persian army. . . .

The scene is Los Angeles; the year is 1974. Without warning, an earthquake has struck, and the great city is literally disintegrating. Huge buildings are crumbling into rubble; freeways are collapsing; dams are giving way; homes are crushed to splinters. . . .

The scene is outer space; the year is 2001. The largest spacecraft ever built has been launched on a mission to Jupiter. Piloted by an intelligent talking computer, with most of its crew in suspended animation, the huge ship sweeps through the black, cold void between planets. . . .

Some of these scenes are real, some imaginary. All have one thing in common: They have been captured forever on film, in movies that really try to live up to the adjectives that are so dear to the hearts of press agents—spectacular, awesome, tremendous, sensational.

From the earliest days of filmmaking, the epic movie has been a staple product and an almost certain guarantee of box-office success. Some epic subjects go on forever, most notably the glory that was Rome. The story of Cleopatra has been told and retold in every movie generation, and the tale of Ben Hur is equally durable. But there are also cycles of interest. In the 1930s, the epic Western movie reached a peak, as Americans became entranced with the winning of the frontier. Later, spectacular movie musicals featuring hundreds of singers and dancers in glorious color were in style. In the 1970s, the disaster movie suddenly became popular, as fans crowded to the box office to see films of earthquakes, fires, disasters at sea and in the air portrayed vividly.

The reason for the popularity of epic films is obvious: Only the movies can show us these great, spectacular scenes, which can only be suggested on a stage and which shrink to absurd tininess on the television screen. Only the movie screen has the size and scope to make the spectacular —the earthquakes, the battles, the parades—really come to life.

It isn't as easy as it may seem, for several reasons. To start with, money alone can't make a spectacular movie; a sense of style and staging is also needed. The history of films is full of stories about movies on which millions of dollars were spent without much being produced to show for it. Anyone can put thousands of extras in costumes on a sound stage, but only a few directors have learned how to make such scenes come through to audiences.

And sometimes even the movies can't spend enough to recreate on the screen what happened in real life. No amount of money could reproduce the real earthquake that destroyed San Francisco in 1905 or the imaginary earthquake that "destroyed" Los Angeles in 1974. Here, imagination and inventiveness come to the rescue. Over the decades, skilled workmen and inventors have developed a bagful of tricks that enable directors to fake almost any scene, from an airplane crash to a forest fire to an earthquake to—you name it, the special effects men of Hollywood and other moviemaking centers can do it.

Other, more physical skills are needed. Someone has to take the falls, go through the auto wrecks, stage the fights, arrange for the airplane crashes, survive the fires. No epic movie ever could be made without calling on the small, tough group of stunt men and women who will do almost anything, however daring, for a fee. Make no mistake about it, their job is truly dangerous; the working life of most stunt people is short, and many have died in attempting a feat that was just too difficult or where the timing was not as precise as had been planned.

Why do it? Money is the obvious reason, but not the only one. There's something both challenging and stimulating about the job—a statement that also applies to epic movies themselves. They appeal to one of the most basic instincts of human beings, to see new places and unusual sights. If you can see those places and sights without the expense and trouble of travel, by just paying at the box office and sitting back in comfort, you will—especially if the film shows you a sight that would otherwise be just a page in the history book: the defense of the Alamo, the sinking of the *Titanic,* the Battle of Bunker Hill, the adventures of Robin Hood in Sherwood Forest. Or you can see a disaster and still know in the back of your mind that it isn't really happening, so you can have your cake and eat it, too.

That's why movie epics will go on forever. Even today, audiences gasp at the amazingly detailed and immense mob scenes made more than a half century ago by D. W. Griffith. And even today, when the movie audience has shrunk to a fraction of its former size because of television, a new epic will still get people out of their living rooms and into the theaters to see what new spectaculars Hollywood has come up with (although, these days, a "Hollywood" film is likely to be an international effort, made far away from the old back lots of the big studios).

The story of movie epics was—and is—an epic story in itself, full of powerful personalities, daredevils who would try almost any stunt, geniuses who could come up with amazingly realistic scenes. It is a story that, in the phrase which was so popular with press agents of old, has "a cast of thousands, years in the making." And this is that story.

"30 Lions, 5,000 People"
The Epic Begins

THE MOVIES DIDN'T WORK up to epic films slowly—they jumped right in feet-first. Just about the first feature-length films made—that is, films that lasted more than a few minutes—were truly epics, relying on huge sets, mob scenes, and spectacular effects to get and hold an audience. What's more, the movie epic was an Italian invention.

In the early 1900s, the people who ran the young but fast-growing movie business in the United States believed that audiences would not have enough patience to see any film longer than one reel, about one thousand feet of film and ten minutes in length. Indeed, when a movie-maker named J. Stuart Blackton made a five-reel story called *The Life of Moses* in 1909, it was released to theaters in sections, just one reel a week.

But, in 1912, when an Italian director named Enrico Guazzoni made a film version of the novel *Quo Vadis?*, a

story set in the time of Christ, he decided to let the
movie run for an unheard-of two hours. In large part,
that was a decision based on sensible business practices.
To make the film, which takes place in ancient Rome,
Guazzoni had to build massive sets and fill them with
hundreds of extras in Roman costume. It seemed foolish
to waste all that on a short movie.

Having made that decision, Guazzoni really spent money
—hiring lions from a circus, horses from the cavalry, wild
animals for the coliseum scenes, and the like. *Quo Vadis?*
was a smash hit, both in Italy and abroad (it played a com-
mand performance for the king of England and movies
jumped their prices when it was shown in the United
States), and the epic film was off and running.

The Roman Empire was an obvious subject for Italian
moviemakers, and so the screen soon saw films about *The
Last Days of Pompeii* ("30 lions, 50 horses, 5,000 people"
the ads screamed) and *Cabiria,* a love story set in Rome and
so successful that it started a string of sequels starring
Maciste, the strong man who rescued Cabiria, the heroine.

In addition to making a lot of money for their backers,
the Italian spectacles also had a powerful influence on an
American named David Wark Griffith, who had already
established himself as one of the best moviemakers in the
United States. In 1913, Griffith made a spectacular titled
Judith of Bethulia, which took place in ancient Assyria,
featured lavish sets and costumes, and clearly owed a lot
to the spectacles made in Italy.

But in 1915, D. W. Griffith made movie history in several ways when he directed *Birth of a Nation.* First, he
produced what is probably the greatest money-maker in
film history; *Birth of a Nation* cost about $100,000 to
make and earned at least $40,000,000—most of that in

the days when a dollar was really a dollar, worth three or four of today's inflated greenbacks. Second, he used the film to perfect many of the techniques of film that have now become standard—close-ups, pan shots, and other imaginative uses of a camera that had been static and stage-bound until then. And third, *Birth of a Nation* gave the U.S. film industry a lead in epics that it has never lost (helped by the fact that World War I dealt a setback to the European movie industry).

Today, *Birth of a Nation* is something of an embarrassment because of its plot, in which the Ku Klux Klan plays a heroic role, the Confederacy is viewed with approval, and opinions now regarded as racist predominate. But individual scenes in the movie, such as Griffith's version of the Civil War Battle of Petersburg (filmed in the San Fernando Valley), are regarded as classics.

Elated with the success of *Birth of a Nation*, Griffith followed it with a movie that he intended to be his masterpiece. Titled *Intolerance*, it had four interrelated stories, one taking place in ancient Babylon, one in the time of Christ, one in seventeenth-century France, and one in modern times, all four designed to show man's inhumanity to man.

For the Babylonian sequence, Griffith built perhaps the most stupendous set ever in movie history. With walls ninety feet high, with carved wooden elephants fifty feet high, with every square inch decorated by skilled workmen and thronged with thousands of extras, the Babylon set still draws gasps from audiences when the film is shown today. (After the film was completed, the set was left to stand for a number of years alongside Sunset Boulevard, a strange sight even in the land of make-believe that was Hollywood.)

The Babylonian set from D. W. Griffith's Intolerance, *still one of the most elaborate in movie history. Note the size of the extras on the wall in the background. (Griffith, 1916)*

Unfortunately, *Intolerance* was a flop. Audiences couldn't follow Griffith's rapid cutting from plot to plot; they didn't get the point he was trying to make and they weren't impressed enough by the spectacular sets and scenes. At the box office, the film bombed.

But it was only a temporary setback for the epic film. Griffith himself went on to make many more, such as *Orphans of the Storm,* about the French Revolution, and *America,* about our War of Independence. And he was joined by many others.

It was a glorious time for Hollywood—the "roaring twenties," when the movie industry entered its first golden era, when box-office receipts increased endlessly, when the first movie stars were created and their salaries went into the stratosphere (by 1926, comedian Harold Lloyd was earning more than $40,000 *a week*), and when studios were ready to pour millions into epics.

Take *Ben Hur,* for example. When Metro-Goldwyn-Mayer decided to make the film in 1925, it first sent an entire unit to Rome to shoot the famous chariot race in the Circus Maximus. But the weather was wrong, so it was back to the United States, where the Circus Maximus was reproduced in Hollywood, filled with four thousand extras (paid $3.50 a day plus lunch), and became the scene of carnage as men and horses were injured to capture an amazingly realistic sequence. The celebrated sea battle was filmed using full-sized vessels that actually were sunk with the extras on board to get the necessary effects.

The sea battle started one of the zaniest stories to come out of Hollywood. Supposedly, the Italian extras working on the film were required to turn in their street clothes at the start of the day. To prevent anyone from being paid more than once, the extras got their clothes and their money when they handed in the costumes at the end of the day. But after the battle scene, someone was shocked to find that more than seventy-five extras had not claimed their clothing. Fearing that they had drowned, the executive ordered the clothing to be disposed of quietly—only to get another shock when the extras, who had been picked up by a passing ship, showed up the next day. Supposedly, the studio had to pay plenty to hush up the episode; like most of the great Hollywood stories, its truth is far from established.

Ben Hur cost an amazing amount of money, some $4,000,000 in all, and the film actually lost money. But it was a sign of the times. Hollywood had really grown up. By the end of the 1920s, the coming of sound transformed the movies forever, but even that change, and the Great Depression that began in 1929, did not stop the boom time in the American film industry.

In the 1930s, the movies were close to their peak. The major studios had hundreds of workmen under contract, and dozens of sound stages busy with continual shooting. Their "back lots" covered acre on acre with almost any set that could be imagined—typical American small towns, dusty Western streets, bustling city scenes, strange foreign locales. For a larger scale, the studios could go "on location" just a few miles away in the San Fernando Valley. And if something really unusual was desired, the studio could whip it up in short order. For example, when MGM wanted to film *Marie Antoinette* in 1939, it built a replica of the ballroom at Versailles that was actually larger than the one built by King Louis IV.

If actors were needed to fill those sets, that was no problem. Central Casting, a co-operative organization

The chariot race from the 1925 version of Ben Hur, *with Ramon Novarro, playing the title role, leading the pack.* (*MGM, 1925*)

founded by the studios, could provide thousands of extras with little notice, and the costume department of the studios could turn those extras into American frontiersmen, English villagers, pirates, soldiers—anything the director's heart desired. To make sure that everything was authentic, the studios kept huge libraries of books and other material, all on call to be certain that the costumes were accurate.

If Hollywood had one fault in that era, it was that the studios hated to get far from home. Their craftsmen were so expert that it seemed foolish to send stars and cameramen far away to shoot footage that could be shot just as well (anyway, almost as well) right on the back lot. If anything was needed to fill in the studio shots, that could be provided by the "second unit," a camera crew under the direction of someone who was skillful, but not yet ready to handle the job of directing a feature film. There were always problems popping up with this arrangement. For example, when Twentieth Century-Fox made *Stanley and Livingstone,* it sent a second unit off to Africa to film the necessary animal shots. The unit included a double who looked like Tyrone Power, who was supposed to play Stanley. But when the second unit was in Africa, the studio changed its mind and signed Spencer Tracy to play Stanley, which meant that much of the film shot in Africa had to be abandoned.

Despite such inevitable embarrassments, the second unit became a necessary part of almost every Hollywood epic. If stunts were to be done, if special footage was to be shot, the second unit could do it without using the valuable time of the stars. Over the years, the second unit became a training ground for many beginners who went on to be major directors and producers, and it also provided work for stunt men and other Hollywood standbys who could use their hard-won film knowledge to good effect in filming backup footage.

What the back lots, the location trips, and the second units could not provide, faking did. Over the years, Hollywood developed a crew of experts who could provide rain, snow, hail, a sunrise, a wind of any force, a natural phenomenon of any type—all at the time and the place the director wanted. Moviemakers also became skilled at handling the huge logistical requirements of the epic films. Electricians, sound men, grips, wardrobe people, special effects people—all are needed to make an epic.

Sometimes split-second timing is required to handle the many elements needed for just one scene in an epic. For example, when the great director King Vidor was filming *War and Peace* in 1954, he had a magnificent idea for introducing the Battle of Borodino: Henry Fonda, playing the hero, Pierre, would pick a flower, then hear a cannon blast and walk over the crest of a hill to see the French and Russian armies move together to clash in the great battle.

Vidor had five thousand infantrymen and eight hundred cavalry to direct (with the help of fifty walkie-talkies), and there were two thousand explosive charges that had to be set off at just the right time to recreate the battle. And he even had to worry about the flower for Fonda to pick!

Here's how it worked: Fonda picked the flower. Word was relayed by radio to special effects men to start the explosions. A few carefully timed seconds later, Fonda came over the hilltop, stepping precisely on a stake driven in to mark his exact place. The Russian and French forces started moving with equal precision. In a little more than a minute,

The battle scene from King Vidor's version of War and Peace. Precise planning was needed to keep the 5,000 extras in the scene going in the right directions. (Paramount, 1956)

the scene had been shot—and that was just one of many scenes needed for the battle in the movie.

With that kind of precision and that many people, small wonder that the million-dollar budget arrived in Hollywood to stay. But Hollywood was willing to spend the money because film epics were big at the box office. For more than two glorious decades, epic after epic rolled off the Hollywood production line. The Hollywood dream factory was in full swing. No one could match American moviemakers at producing these giant films, half fact and half fantasy, and the public seemed ready to watch anything that Hollywood wanted to produce. It was the golden era of epics.

The Great Cecil B.
(and Others)

THE STORY GOES LIKE THIS: Director Cecil B. DeMille, filming *The Ten Commandments*, was ready to shoot the scene showing the flight of the Hebrews from Egypt. The set was full of action—thousands of extras dressed as Hebrews or as Egyptian soldiers, hundreds of animals, from camels to donkeys to steeds harnessed to war chariots. Three cameras had been set up to capture the action as DeMille signaled the scene to start—a scene followed by frenzied action as actors and animals went through their well-rehearsed paces.

When the scene was over, DeMille turned to the first cameraman. "Gee, Mr. DeMille," the man said, "I'm sorry to tell you that the film jammed." So DeMille went to the second camera. "Sorry, Mr. DeMille, but I had trouble getting the camera lens off," was the response. Finally, DeMille turned desperately to the third camera, high on a hilltop overlooking the scene. In response to his frantic waves,

The Ten Commandments, *in Cecil B. DeMille's first ver-*
sion, made as a silent film in 1923. The huge scale of the sets
and the lavish use of extras were typical of a DeMille produc-
tion. (*Paramount, 1923*)

DeMille got an answer from the third cameraman: "Ready whenever you are, C.B."

The story probably isn't true, but it is fitting that such a tale should be told of Cecil B. DeMille. For, unquestionably, DeMille was Hollywood's king of the epic film.

No one ever made as many epics as gaudily as the great DeMille, and no one was as consistently successful in making epics come to life. The critics could (and did) laugh at DeMille's simple, usually corny, plots; they could make fun of his manhandling of historical facts. (When he did *Unconquered,* about colonial America, Colonel George Washington predictably showed up for a brief chat with the hero; in any film DeMille made about the Civil War era, Abraham Lincoln was certain to appear.) But no one could argue with DeMille's ability to come up with just the right touch to make an ordinarily spectacular scene really come alive.

Things like having Claudette Colbert take a bath in milk in *The Sign of the Cross,* filmed in 1932 (the milk was heavily loaded with lard to imitate cream, and soon stank to high heaven under the hot studio lights), having zebras draw Mary Magdalene's chariot in *King of Kings* (1927), having the Red Sea part realistically in *The Ten Commandments* (made twice by DeMille, once in 1923, once in 1956) and then swallow up the Egyptian army—all of these were the true signs of the DeMille form of genius, which could make audiences accept scenes that would have produced only unbelieving laughs if handled by just about any other director.

For subject matter, DeMille zigzagged from ancient Rome to the Bible to American history, with a heavy concentration on the winning of the West. His career, which started in the earliest days of Hollywood, at first was filled with light bedroom comedies. The first version of *The Ten Commandments* was DeMille's start in the epic-film area, and even though it cost $1,600,000, a huge budget for those days, it made a lot of money for Paramount Pictures. Four years later, DeMille made *King of Kings,* a reverent telling of the Christ story (DeMille insisted that the actors not drink, smoke, or gamble during the production of the film) that was also highly profitable. From then on, the epic film was the DeMille specialty—such films as *Cleopatra,* made in 1934 and starring Claudette Colbert, which many fans still think superior to the later Elizabeth Taylor version, even though DeMille filmed in black and white on a tight budget; *Union Pacific* (1939), about the building of the transcontinental railroad and featuring, among other scenes, a grand Indian attack on a train; *Northwest Mounted Police,* made in 1940 and starring Gary Cooper as a Texas Ranger come to Canada to track down a killer; and *Reap the Wild Wind* (1940), which had an impressively realistic giant octopus attacking a deep-sea diver.

Probably the one film in which DeMille was in his fullest glory was the 1956 version of *The Ten Commandments,* which starred Charlton Heston as a muscular Moses and Yul Brynner as a suitably wicked Pharaoh (although a few DeMille fans hold out for *Samson and Delilah,* made in 1949, which had Hedy Lamarr as Delilah, Victor Mature as Samson, and a finale in which the temple destruction was resplendently done). Filmed in glorious color, featuring just about every extra that could be rounded up and marked by such attention to detail as having Anne Baxter's gown painstakingly reproduce an Egyptian wall painting, filmed on location in Egypt with sets that recreated the ancient temples of that land, the film got cries of pain from most critics, but drew moviegoers

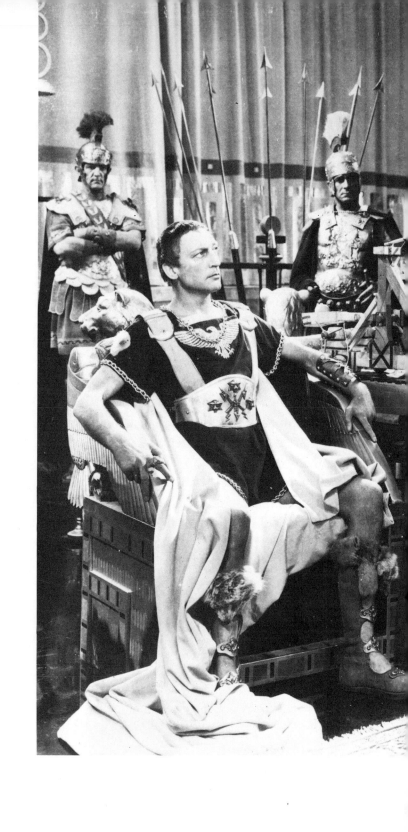

The DeMille touch: Claudette Colbert and Warren William (seated) in DeMille's Cleopatra. *(Paramount, 1934)*

The Ten Commandments, *made by DeMille again in 1956, this time in color and sound, but with the same DeMille lavishness. (Paramount, 1956)*

A 1950s epic: The Roman triumph scene from Quo Vadis? (MGM, 1951)

in droves, earning more than $40,000,000 at the box office.
DeMille died three years later, still the acknowledged king
of spectacular films.

Success such as that naturally attracted the attention of
other moviemakers, and there were always other epics
being produced—some as good as DeMille's, some better,
some not in the same league.

The *Ben Hur* of the 1920s has already been mentioned.
There was also *Noah's Ark* of 1928, whose production
was marred by tragedy when three extras drowned while
shooting the flood scene. In Europe, *Quo Vadis?* was
made in 1924, and *Last Days of Pompeii* was produced
in 1926.

Obviously, the Roman Empire—particularly the Roman
era that saw the rise of Christianity—has been a popular
theme of epic makers; so much so that they keep coming
back to the same stories. *Ben Hur*, filmed in silent black
and white in 1927, was filmed in color in 1960, starring
Charlton Heston, winning an Academy Award, and notable more for such scenes as the chariot race and the
battle at sea than for its acting or drama. *Quo Vadis?*
was remade in the United States in 1951, starring Robert
Taylor, Deborah Kerr, and Peter Ustinov as a decadent
Nero; again, the sheer size and expense of the film was
the most impressive part of the production.

It took the British to make two spectacles that won the
applause of the critics (although the films did not do
overwhelmingly well at the box office) and, amazingly,
both these epics were made during the pinched days of
World War II, when the British had few resources to spare
for moviemaking. One of the epics was *Caesar and Cleopatra*, a film version of the play by George Bernard Shaw,
which still is believed to be the most expensive film ever

made in Britain. Claude Rains (as Caesar) and Vivien Leigh (as Cleopatra) were excellent, the sets were stunning (although much of the budget never showed on the screen, since the money was spent to isolate the production from the noise and shock of the war outside), and the supporting cast was equally good. Unfortunately, those who liked the Shaw play thought the movie was too lavish, and those who liked epics did not go for Shaw's play, so the movie never really made it.

The other successful epic was Laurence Olivier's version of Shakespeare's *Henry V*. Olivier, one of the great actors of our time, played the lead role and directed a talented cast of British actors whose work made the film one of the best movie versions of any Shakespeare play. And for sheer spectacle, the scene where the French knights, brilliant in their armor and plumes, come charging down at the battle of Agincourt to be met by a devastating flight of arrows from the thin line of English longbowmen has rarely been equaled on the screen. It is said that the film, with its story of an outnumbered English army victorious against all odds, helped to rally that battered nation for the last effort of World War II.

But those were the exceptions among the costume epics. For the most part, the toga-and-chariot epics never really amounted to much of artistic merit, even though their financial success kept Hollywood turning them out. One success led to another. *The Robe*, a 1953 version of Lloyd C. Douglas' novel about the aftermath of Christ's crucifixion (and, incidentally, the first film made in Cinemascope), led two years later to a sequel, *Demetrius and the Gladiator*, which bored the critics as much as it thrilled the fans. There was *The Silver Chalice*, with Paul Newman and Virginia Mayo not being very convincing about ancient

Part of the spectacular battle scene from Henry V, a movie which showed that Shakespeare on the screen can be exciting. (Rank, 1944)

Rome, *David and Bathsheba, Solomon and Sheba*—well, you get the idea.

But the Bible and Rome were not the only inspirations for spectacular films. Hollywood had learned a profitable lesson: Anything that could be advertised as bigger and grander had an excellent chance of making money. And so almost anything could be turned into an epic.

Dancing Girls, Cowboys, and Swashbucklers

Yes, there were epic musicals, too, and the man who made most of them in the early days was Busby Berkeley. Of course, before there could be movie musicals there had to be sound in the movies, something that didn't happen until *The Jazz Singer* was released in 1927. There had been some attempts to make the movies speak before then, but *The Jazz Singer*, which had Al Jolson singing (which made it the first musical) and talking a few words, revolutionized the movie industry.

Busby Berkeley came to Hollywood in 1929, from a successful career on Broadway. After working on the musical numbers for some pictures at Warner Brothers, Berkeley moved to Metro-Goldwyn-Mayer, where he began doing things with the camera that no musical director had ever done before.

If one thing was the Busby Berkeley trademark, it was a camera shot from high above the action, showing the dancers and chorus girls moving in marvelous patterns. As

Berkeley told it, the idea for that shot came to him one day at Warner Brothers when he climbed into the rafters to look at one of his numbers, was impressed with the view, and said to himself, "I better bring the audience up here and let them see it." To do that, he literally had to cut a hole in the roof of the sound stage, but the results fascinated movie audiences and quickly set a style for the whole decade of the 1930s.

Shooting from above, Berkeley had his chorus girls go through precision routines that gave marvelous images of changing patterns, resembling the sights seen through a kaleidoscope. The straight-down camera angle was so popular that it was quickly imitated by many directors who didn't have Berkeley's imagination, and so it quickly became a laughable cliché. But in its early days, the new camera angle was an eye opener.

It wasn't just the "top shot" that made Busby Berkeley musicals so spectacular—it was a zany kind of imagination that used the camera as few directors had dared to use it before. In *42nd Street*, a musical he made for MGM in 1933, Berkeley started the big number by showing Ruby Keeler, the star, doing a solo dance. As the camera pulls back, the audience sees that she is dancing on top of a taxicab, and that the taxicab is parked in the middle of 42nd Street. From that point, the number gets bigger and bigger. In the film, the number is supposed to be part of a Broadway musical, but no stage could hold the spectacular mass of scenery and dancers that Berkeley used.

That was true of most of his best-known numbers, which could have been made only by the movies. Anything went in a Busby Berkeley musical. For the "By a Waterfall" spectacular in *Footlight Parade*, he built an aquacade that used hydraulic lifts to move one hundred

The "By a Waterfall" scene from Busby Berkeley's Footlight Parade, *which featured lots of chorus girls, lots of water, and unusual camera angles.* (Warner Brothers, 1933)

chorus girls, and had 20,000 gallons of water pumped every minute as the girls tumbled down into a studio-built lake.

For *Gold Diggers of 1931*, Berkeley had one number that started with the camera zooming in on a singer, whose profile turned into a city skyline, the prelude for one of his huge production numbers. For *Gold Diggers of 1935*, Berkeley had one hundred girls sitting at one hundred pianos—and the pianos danced while the girls sat still. All of this was expensive, an estimated $10,000 for every minute of film, but it was worth it at the box office.

The piano scene from Gold Diggers of 1935. *Busby Berkeley had the girls sit still while the pianos danced. (Warner Brothers, 1935)*

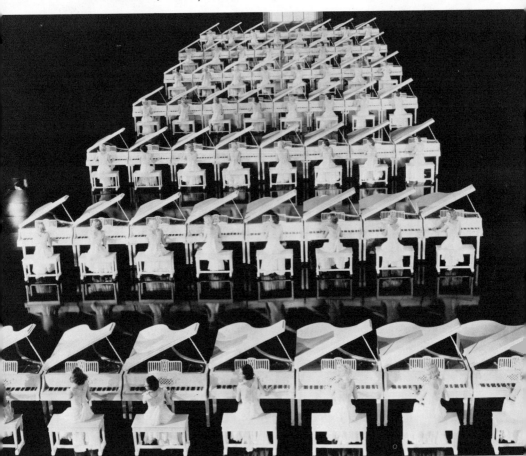

Naturally, this kind of success invited imitation, and the screen soon was crowded with musical films in which the production numbers were filled with mobs of dancing girls, top-hatted chorus boys, incredibly complicated sets, and unusual camera angles. But this didn't last very long, for one reason: In spite of all his imagination and inventiveness, the films that Busby Berkeley made weren't really very good. The plots usually were ridiculous (almost always involving a simple chorus girl who became a star overnight in an unbelievable way) and even the spectacular production numbers began to get yawns after audiences had seen a dozen or so of them. Today, when people talk about the great musicals of the 1930s, they usually mean Fred Astaire movies. Those may have had some spectacular scenes, but mostly they just featured Fred Astaire and Ginger Rogers dancing by themselves as no other team has ever danced.

The same is true of the musicals of the 1940s and 1950s, when color was added to the spectaculars. The bloated musicals that were clogged with dozens of stars and hundreds of dancers who went through the epic production numbers had their day and now are mostly forgotten. What people remember, and what comes back to revival theaters today, are simpler films, such as *Meet Me in St. Louis*, starring Judy Garland in a touching story of an ordinary American family, or *The Band Wagon*, which spoofed spectacular musicals and which succeeded because its big numbers were down to earth.

True, a lot of money was spent on many of the later color musicals, and to good effect. Spectacular scenes such as the finale in *Singin' in the Rain* and the "American in Paris" ballet in *American in Paris* cost plenty, but they are remembered not because of the money but because they were done

in unforgettable style. Indeed, the one number from *Singin'
in the Rain* that most people remember was the title song,
which had Gene Kelly dancing all by himself on a rain-
drenched street. And these days, some critics complain that
the "American in Paris" ballet does not stand up as well as
the other numbers from that great musical.

Fortunately for those who were too young to see the
musicals on their first time around, MGM released a fine
anthology of its best in a 1974 film called *That's Entertainment*, which had a great selection of the best of
Hollywood musicals, and which became one of the box-
office smashes of the year. It turned out that the old musicals looked just as good the second time around as they
did the first time. In fact, they looked so much better
than most of the 1970s films that older fans got weepily
nostalgic about the good old days, which they didn't ap-
preciate at the time.

The same story could be told about the Hollywood
Westerns: Few people realized how good they were until
their great days were over. And just as Busby Berkeley
was the major figure in the epic musical, there was an
equally towering figure in the epic Western: John Ford,
who started directing Westerns in 1917 and continued in
a career that spanned more than fifty years and that was
full of movies now acknowledged to be masterpieces.

There was one big difference between Busby Berkeley
and John Ford: Most of Berkeley's films were not worth
much outside of their big production numbers. Most of
John Ford's movies are worth seeing as movies, pure and
simple. There are plenty of fans around who are ready to
say that Ford's production of *Stagecoach* is still the best
Western ever made, even though it dates back to 1939
and has been outdone technically by many other films.

It wasn't sheer size and numbers that made Ford's Westerns epic movies. Many other directors, notably Cecil B. DeMille in his Western productions, could turn out more Indians, cowboys, or cattle for a big scene. But Ford had a real feeling for the land and its people, whites and Indians, that came through to give the audience the feeling of an epic. No one has ever been better than Ford at using the West itself—its plains, its cliffs, its valleys—as an epic backdrop for drama, and no one has been better at maneuvering horsemen against these monumental natural settings. Finally, Ford had a long and productive relationship with John Wayne, who starred in most of the best Ford Westerns and who now is recognized as being the greatest Western star of them all—not because he is the best actor ever to appear in Westerns or because people agree with his politics, but because he seems to sum up all the feelings, good and bad, that Americans have ever had about the West.

Of course, John Ford wasn't the only director to make epic Westerns. For the record, the first truly epic Western was *The Covered Wagon,* a silent film directed by James Cruze in 1923. *The Covered Wagon* is regarded as a rather slow and tame movie today, but it was a sensation in its time, and it established the popularity of the Western in Hollywood for good. After the release of *The Covered Wagon,* the number of Westerns filmed in Hollywood jumped, and the increase proved to be permanent. Big Westerns, little Westerns, singing Westerns, epic Westerns—Hollywood turned them out by the score.

Some are worth mention: *Cimarron,* which won the Academy Award in 1931 and featured a spectacular land-rush scene recreating the day when the Indian Territory was thrown open for settlers. Director Wesley Ruggles

The Covered Wagon, *a silent film that was the first West-ern epic. The wagons are in a circle for an Indian attack.* (*Paramount, 1923*)

sent hundreds of wagons, horses, and riders careening across the prairie for the scene. DeMille's *The Plainsman* of 1936 starred Gary Cooper as Wild Bill Hickok and Jean Arthur as Calamity Jane in a very long movie. *Dodge City,* made in 1939, was noteworthy as Errol Flynn's first Western and for having what is probably the most spectacular brawl ever put on film: a whole saloon filled wall to wall with cowboys smashing bottles, tables, chairs, and fists against each other.

John Ford made *Stagecoach* the same year. He went to Monument Valley, located in a Navaho reservation on the border between Utah and Arizona; a desert with steep hills towering above it, beautiful to see and beautifully photographed by Ford. *Stagecoach,* which put a motley group of passengers in a coach for a long ride that was climaxed by (a) a marvelous Indian chase which ended (naturally) in a last-minute rescue and (b) a shootout between hero John Wayne and the villains in a Western town, made Wayne a star. It remains a grand movie, much better than a feeble remake released in 1966.

Some other Westerns that rate as real epics: *Western Union* (1941), which showed how the telegraph was strung across the prairie and included a great scene in which the company's camp burned down; *They Died with Their Boots On* (1941), which starred Errol Flynn as a heroic George Armstrong Custer and which ended with an epic filming of the Battle of the Little Big Horn (thirty years later, Dustin Hoffman was to star in *Little Big Man,* a film that showed the Indians as heroes and depicted Custer as a raving lunatic); *Shane* (1953), starring Alan Ladd as the laconic hero, with director George Stevens doing a great job of using the plains and mountains as a huge backdrop for a tiny Western town; *Red River*

(1948), in which John Wayne first played a middle-aged man and in which director Howard Hawks had one of the best cattle stampedes ever put on film; *How the West Was Won* (1963), notable now because it was the first (and one of the few) Western in Cinerama; and so on.

In fact, and so on and on and on. The fashion in heroes may have changed, and these days moviemakers may like to show the seamy side of the West—the dirt and gore that they once preferred to ignore—but the Western obviously will go on forever. If you think about it, it is curious to note that the idea of the West in most Americans' minds comes not from reality but from the West of the movies, and usually of the epic movies. In pretending to record history, the epic Westerns actually made history by changing the way Americans viewed the West. We used to see the settlers and the cowboys and the cavalry as heroic; now the Indians are having their day. The view may change again in the future, but you can be sure that there will be more epic Westerns made to reflect that new view.

In the same way, Hollywood in the golden era gave Americans the same peculiar view of another history—the history of Europe, which, on the silver screen, became a place of pirates and cavaliers, of thrilling sea battles and endless duels. Rewriting the real story with more imagination than credibility, Hollywood created a series of epic swashbuckling romances that today would be laughed off the screen by audiences but, in decades gone by, hit just the right note.

It wasn't a director who stood out in the swashbuckling films but an actor: Errol Flynn, the Irish-born leading man (already mentioned as a hero of Westerns), who had a perfect profile, just the right trace of British accent

Captain Blood, *Errol Flynn's first big starring role, a movie swarming with extras and cutlasses. (Warner Brothers, 1935)*

in his voice, and the flair to carry off almost any romantic plot, no matter how absurd it might be.

There was Errol Flynn as *Captain Blood*, his first major film, made in 1935, leading an escape from a convict island and then becoming "the greatest pirate captain on the Spanish Main"; Errol Flynn leading *The Charge of the Light Brigade* in a 1936 movie that had a preposterous plot which somehow spent most of its time in India instead of the Ukraine where the fighting took place (but which also had a magnificent finale, a charge of the Light Brigade that was almost unbearably exciting—and that took a great toll of horses and stunt men); Errol Flynn as the bandit of Sherwood Forest in *The Adventures of Robin Hood* (1938), one of the best costume adventure films that Hollywood ever made; Errol Flynn in the title role of *The Sea Hawk* (1940), playing the favorite captain of Queen Elizabeth and (of course) managing to turn back the Spanish Armada almost singlehanded; Errol Flynn as the Earl of Essex in *Elizabeth and Essex* (1939), playing the doomed lover of Queen Elizabeth . . .

The roles went on and on, and the fans loved it. These swashbuckling adventures rewrote history to a shocking degree, but nobody really cared whether or not they were historically accurate. They were just great fun, full of romantic love scenes, dashing adventures by the hero (who always could outfight any three, four, or five opponents), and mob scenes swarming with soldiers, sailors, pirates, knights, or what have you. One thing was always the same: The final scene always came down to a dramatic swordfight between the hero and the villain—up stairs, over balconies, through great halls, with the villain always getting skewered at the end in a highly improbable way. Sometimes he went over the battlements of a castle, sometimes he died at the feet of a queen, sometimes he toppled into a moat; you could count on an appropriately gruesome end for the villain just in time for the hero and heroine to clinch at the fadeout.

Naturally, Errol Flynn wasn't the only star of swash-buckling epics. There were plenty of great swashbucklers starring other actors—for example, *The Prisoner of Zenda,* made in 1937 and starring Ronald Colman in the double role of the king and the commoner who took his place after a kidnaping. *The Prisoner of Zenda* was full of epic scenes—a ball in the palace with hundreds of waltzing couples, the coronation in a crowded cathedral—and its final duel between Colman and Douglas Fairbanks, Jr., is one of the best ever done. *The Prisoner of Zenda* was done again in 1952, starring Stewart Granger, in a version that was not quite up to the previous film. *The Scarlet Pimpernel,* made in England in 1938, had Leslie Howard as a British nobleman who pretended to be weak and lazy so he could help prisoners escape from the Terror of the French Revolution. *The Thief of Baghdad,* made in 1940, was a Technicolor swashbuckler set in a never-never land of ancient Arabia, with remarkable special effects—a genie who popped from a bottle and grew to giant size, a flying carpet, a winged horse, and many other wonders. *Scaramouche,* made in 1952 and starring Stewart Granger, was a swashbuckler set in the France of Revolutionary times, filmed with an unusual sense of humor, and featuring a marvelous final duel through the boxes, stage, and seats of a theater.

The list could go on and on, but it is a list of past glories. Errol Flynn died in 1959, but the swashbuckling epic had died before him. Somewhere along the line, the standard plot of these costume epics, and the standard set of characters—the heroine as pure as the driven snow, the hero stronger than anyone else, the villain as wicked as the devil—became too simple-minded for audiences. Some of the final costume epics were among the best—*The Crimson Pirate* (1952) and *The Flame and the Arrow* (1950), both starring Burt Lancaster doing incredible acrobatics—but audiences just wouldn't buy it any more. They wanted more realism—more gore, more nastiness, more complications. And Hollywood, always listening to the music of money at the box office, was ready to give the public exactly what it wanted.

Disaster!

IT REALLY STARTED WITH *The Poseidon Adventure,* the 1972 film that had an ocean liner turning upside down under the impact of a giant wave, and then followed the adventures of a band of passengers trying to fight their way upward to safety. The critics universally disliked the movie, calling its characters absurd and its plot ridiculous, but audiences loved it so much that it took in an impressive $162,000,000 at the box office. With that kind of money to be made, the great disaster race of the 1970s was off to a running start.

There had been plenty of movies in past years featuring disasters: for example, *San Francisco,* made in 1936 and starring Clark Gable and Jeanette MacDonald, which had a final earthquake sequence that, one reviewer reported, showed "walls caving, bricks pouring, houses toppling, streets gaping, and a city burning." But although these scenes could be long (the *San Francisco* earthquake lasted twenty minutes on the screen), they were always

Disaster strikes in The Poseidon Adventure, *a movie whose success started a wave of disaster movies. (Twentieth Century-Fox, 1972)*

just one part of the movie's plot. The disaster films of the 1970s were different because their disasters were the whole point of the plot.

For some reason, maybe because the world no longer seemed to be a very cheerful, hopeful place, the movie audiences of the 1970s were in a mood to pay for seeing terrible things—earthquakes, fires, airplane crashes, explosions, and what they did to people. And even though the biggest stars in the movies were in the disaster films, the focus of these films was not so much on the characters as on the disasters themselves.

The best of the lot was *The Towering Inferno*, which was produced by Irwin Allen, the same man who made *The Poseidon Adventure*. *Inferno* was built around a fire that took place in a (imaginary) 138-floor San Francisco skyscraper, supposedly the world's tallest, and the various miseries that the fire caused to people in the tower.

The film got its title in a particularly Hollywoodian way. Warner Brothers bought the movie rights to a book called *The Tower*, and Twentieth Century-Fox bought the movie rights to a book called *The Glass Inferno*. Realizing that they were working on almost identical films, the two studios agreed to pool their resources for a joint production—it had never been done before—and came up with a title including both books. The critics all said the same thing: The plot of the movie didn't really matter, because the only thing worth seeing was the fire and the firefighters. The audiences? They bought tickets.

Aside from the fire, there were plenty of stars to see: Steve McQueen, Paul Newman, William Holden, Faye Dunaway, Fred Astaire, even football hero O. J. Simpson making his acting debut in films. And there was plenty of disaster, too: people falling from the building, a helicop-

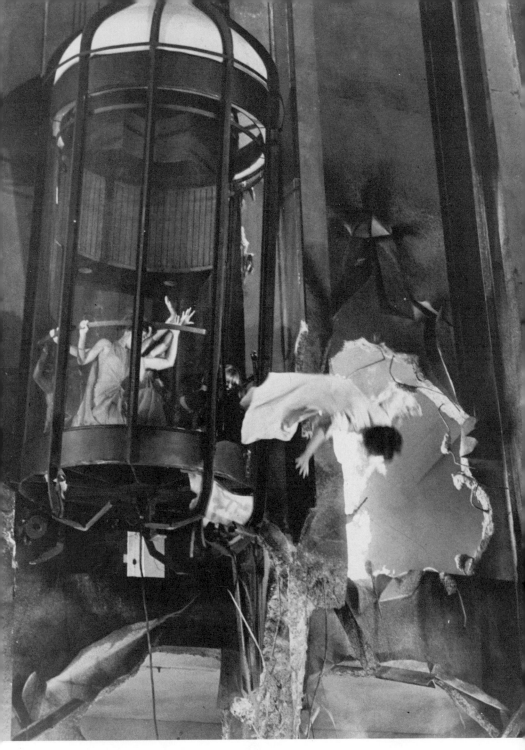

More disaster in The Towering Inferno, *with hapless victims trying to escape from a blaze in the world's tallest skyscraper. (Twentieth Century-Fox, 1974)*

ter crashing, fire licking at human bodies. And then the grand finale—Newman, who played the architect, and McQueen, who played the fire chief, fighting their way to the top of the building to explode a water tank, sending millions of gallons of water cascading down to put out the fire.

Needless to say, the owners of modern office buildings were very unhappy with *The Towering Inferno.* Indeed, an owners' group asked Irwin Allen, the producer, to put a disclaimer at the start of the film, saying that such a disaster could not happen. Irwin said he would do that only if they put a plaque in every modern office building saying, "This Building Is Not Fireproof"—an offer they politely declined. Irwin said he had done research indicating that many new office buildings did not have the necessary equipment for fighting fires that broke out in their upper floors—and sure enough, only months after the release of *The Towering Inferno,* there was a major fire that gutted six floors of the World Trade Center in New York, exactly the kind of skyscraper that the movie was about. The World Trade Center fire, fortunately, was not anywhere near the disaster depicted in the film; however, it did disclose many of the weaknesses in skyscraper defenses against fire that were shown in *The Towering Inferno.*

That was one major reason for the success of the disaster films: They were about the kind of disasters that were in the news in the 1970s. For example, *Airport,* made in 1970 (and not quite in the disaster film category, although it certainly was an epic), was built around the crisis that occurs when an unbalanced passenger smuggles a bomb on board a crowded jetliner—and the movie came out when airliner hijackings and bomb threats

seemed to be in the headlines every day. *Airport 1975,*
the sequel, was a true disaster picture (and, the critics
said, a disaster as a picture) that was based on a midair
collision between a private airplane and a jumbo jetliner
—and it came out in the midst of publicity about the weaknesses of the air safety system in the United States.

As for *Earthquake,* which was the major competitor to
The Towering Inferno in the disaster film sweepstakes,
that movie was based on an event that most people in
Southern California dread but try not to think about—a
major earthquake in the heart of the nation's second most
populous city, Los Angeles. Just a few years earlier, in
1971, a fairly sizable quake had occurred in the San Fernando Valley, killing sixty-four people and causing more
than half a billion dollars in property damage as hundreds of buildings (including some labeled as quake-proof)
were wrecked, freeways collapsed, and dams threatened to
give way. It didn't take much stretching of the imagination
for Jennings Lang, executive producer of the movie (who
had almost been knocked out of bed when the 1971 quake
hit his home), to scale up the relatively mild San Fernando
earthquake, put its center in downtown Los Angeles, and
then picture its effect on hillside homes, towering skyscrap-
ers, crowded freeways, and reservoirs.

Geologists agree that the effects of such a quake on
Los Angeles would be disastrous, and since the city, like
San Francisco, sits near major geological faults (cracks in
the earth's crust where quakes most often occur), the sci-
entists also agree that such an earthquake is always a
possibility. So seeing the movie is like living a nightmare
for Californians, while moviegoers in the rest of the country can get that odd thrill that comes from viewing someone else's troubles.

Los Angeles isn't really in ruins in this scene from Earth-quake, which uses a combination of photographs, paintings, and steam to create the effect. (Universal, 1975)

And just in case the sight of a city collapsing was not enough to draw crowds, the makers of *Earthquake* came up with a gimmick they called Sensurround, which tried to give the feeling of an earthquake by using low-frequency sound waves. If a sound is deep enough, humans don't hear it; they feel it. So the makers of *Earthquake* used bass tones below the normal range of human hearing, amplified them as much as possible, and broadcast them in the theater through the most powerful loudspeakers available. As Los Angeles came tumbling down on the screen, the audience was supposed to literally shake in its seats. Dozens of theaters agreed to install the special equipment needed for Sensurround; because the sound waves are potentially dangerous to weak structures, theaters had to have a special architectural checkup before they were allowed to provide this extra thrill.

If that still wasn't enough, *Earthquake* finished on a high note of disaster, a bursting dam that just about wiped the ruins of Los Angeles off the map. Not since *The Rains Came*, a 1939 film starring Tyrone Power that put *its* climactic earthquake and flood in India, had the screen seen such well-done natural destruction. In years to come, there probably will be an endless debate about which is better, the earthquake-flood in *Earthquake*, or the earthquake-flood in *The Rains Came* (which was remade, not as well, in 1955 under the title of *The Rains of Ranchipur*).

There won't be much debate about which is the better movie. Without its earthquake, *Earthquake* would have no reason to be. Without *its* earthquake, *The Rains Came* still has interesting characters and a good plot. But the movie business is a business, and if people will pay to see epic disaster pure and simple, Hollywood will give them that, just as Hollywood once gave them epic costume dramas and epic musicals and epic Westerns.

So the 1970s saw *Juggernaut*, a disaster epic about a bomb plot on an ocean liner and *Hindenburg*, an epic built around a recreation of the spectacular fire that destroyed the dirigible in 1937, and other disaster epics as well. The reviews of these films, and the audience reaction, tended to be the same: great disaster scenes, not-so-great scenes when the actors began acting instead of running for their lives. In other words, the special effects carried the films.

There was a bright side to that reaction for at least one part of the movie industry—the special effects sections, which had been fading away until the disaster epics came along to revive them. In the golden age of Hollywood, the big studios all had huge special effects departments that could create almost any scene, from an earthquake to a chariot race to an airplane duel to a medieval tournament to a forest fire, all on relatively short notice and at a minimum of cost. The trend to "realistic" films in the 1960s put many of these skilled workmen out of a job. Now they are back at work again, with the help of skilled stunt men and women, making movie magic in all the old ways and adding new tricks of the trade that allow Hollywood to bring to life just about any scene, real or imaginary, past, present, or future.

How Did They Do That?

WHEN METRO-GOLDWYN-MAYER MADE *An American in Paris* in 1951, the only people from the studio who went to Paris were members of a second unit that shot some street scenes to use as backgrounds. Everything else was done right on the MGM lot. The studio built three full-sized Parisian streets, as realistic as anyone could ask, including a café where much of the action took place. The streets were filled with Parisian pedestrians and vehicles; by changing the lighting, the scene could go from day to night in a few minutes. When the River Seine was needed for a dreamy scene with the stars, Gene Kelly and Leslie Caron, set designers came up with a lifelike Seine that was just three inches deep, with a bridge and Notre Dame cathedral in the background painted on a backdrop that was 160 feet long and 35 feet high.

It was all convincing enough to help the film win the Academy Award that year, but the magic done for *An American in Paris* is just one rather mild example of what

Hollywood's set builders and special effects wizards can do. They can take an audience anywhere on (or off) the earth at any time in history. They use incredibly detailed models, unusual camera techniques, a battery of machines, large and small, that can create any phenomenon of the weather. They use double exposures and hidden wires and unorthodox film speeds and trained animals and special lights and distorting lenses. Most of all, they use imagination, without which all the technical tricks would not be effective at all.

Special effects are just about as old as the movies themselves. Many of the techniques used for the crucial scenes of the latest disaster films go back to the earliest days of hand-cranked cameras and silent films. Take the "glass shot," which can be used to create an impressive set without spending much money. The principle is simple: a scene, or part of it, is painted on a sheet of glass, and the camera shoots the action through the glass.

A glass shot is one way of adding extra floors to a building or such things as mountains or trees to a background. Just paint the extra floors, the mountains or the trees on the glass, position the glass so that the added scenery fits in properly with the real scenery, and the audience will never know the difference. However, the glass shot has its faults. The camera cannot move, and the actors must be positioned so they don't walk behind the painted part of the glass, which would destroy the illusion. But because the glass shot is so cheap, it was especially popular in the earliest days of the movies, when budgets were at their stingiest.

It was in those early days, when the century was in its teens, that another basic technique of the special effects department got its start. This was back projection, which is simple in principle. A semitransparent screen is set up, and film of a scene is projected onto the screen. The image comes through the screen, and the actors do their work in front of the image. As a result, you can have actors in Hollywood doing a scene with a real African background, even though none of the actors has ever seen Africa. The resulting "process shot," if handled with care, will fool almost anyone.

But there are problems with back projection, too. One of them is technical, caused by the fact that movie film goes through the camera and the projector at the rate of twenty-four frames a second. The camera that is filming the actors must be synchronized precisely with the projector that is showing the background, or the method just doesn't work. And because the scene being projected on the screen is not as bright as the real-life actors, great care must be used in setting light levels or the sense of realism is lost.

It was not until the 1930s that these and other problems were mastered, but then the process shot quickly became a Hollywood mainstay. It was an era when Hollywood's moguls preferred to stay right at home to make their movies, and so most of the films of the time used process shots, sometimes in a majority of scenes, and in ways that stretched the idea to its limit. In Cecil B. DeMille's 1936 Western epic, *The Plainsman,* for example, the big final battle between the cowboys and the Indians was a process shot. The cowboys were in the studio and the Indians were on film, having been filmed by a second unit in the West some time before. And in *The Wizard of Oz,* the 1939 film that made Judy Garland a star, the scene in which Dorothy is carried off to Oz in a tornado had Judy and her dog in a house, looking out the window at a rear projection that had such improbable things as a rowboat and a woman on a bicycle flying through the air. Sometimes the moviemakers would even have live actors carrying on a conversation with other actors on film in a process shot!

Another basic technique of special effects that goes back to the earliest days and is still widely used is the matte shot, which involves putting the film through the camera more than once. In its simplest form, the matte shot has the cameraman filming a scene with part of the scenery blacked out by a card, called a matte. Then the partially exposed film goes into another camera, which films a scene that fills in the blacked-out area. The combination produces a new scene—for example, actors in the foreground, mountains in the background, each filmed separately. A matte shot is one way of allowing an actor to play a double role in a single scene. (Another method is to use a split screen, exposing the right half of the film the first time through, and the left half the second time.)

The problem with the original mattes was that they could only be used with stationary backgrounds. But soon several ingenious methods were developed for "traveling mattes," in which live action can be combined with moving backgrounds. In one of the earliest versions, the appropriate parts of the film were blacked out by hand, laboriously, frame by frame—a technique that still can be used for scenes where very close interaction between the actors and the background is needed. If you see a shot of a building collapsing on a crowd of extras (for example, such as the falling skyscraper in *Earthquake*), a hand-drawn traveling matte probably has been used, combining shots of a miniature building with real people. But most traveling mattes today are made by using complex lighting techniques and then manipulating the exposed film. By filming a scene using, say, sodium vapor lights, which emit yellow light, to illuminate the background but not the actors, appropriate development tricks can produce a strip of film with the desired traveling matte.

An essential ingredient in producing the final product using matte shots is something called the optical printer, which is a special camera that takes a frame-by-frame picture of a strip of film. It is the optical printer that allows moviemakers to combine exposures for successful matte shots. Sometimes, for especially complicated special effects, a scene will be put through the optical printer ten or twelve times, each round adding one more element, until the desired effect is achieved. Because the results are so satisfactory, the traveling matte today is used for most of the effects that once would have utilized process shots.

In recent years, a new camera technique has come along —front projection. This method had a peculiar origin—it started with a material developed by the Minnesota Mining and Manufacturing Company for road signs and automobile-bumper stickers. This material uses an enormous number of plastic beads—about a million to the square inch—and it has the valuable property of reflecting with great intensity any light that shines on it. (You've probably seen the reflection from this material when driving at night.)

Front projection is like back projection except that the filmed background is projected in front of the camera by a somewhat weak projector. The actors perform in front of a screen made of the special reflective material. Because the projector is weak, you can't see the projected background image on them. And because the reflective screen is so effective, the camera does pick up that image very well. And so the scene that goes down on film shows the actors in a place where they probably have never been before. A scene that uses front projection probably will look more realistic to an audience than a scene that uses back projection, because the front-projected scene does not have the loss of clarity that comes with being shown through a semitransparent screen. First perfected in the 1960s, front projection now is a standard movie method.

In addition to all these camera techniques, the special effects department also has a variety of other methods available to it. One such method is animation—the same animation that is used to create movie cartoons. If a director wants to show something that cannot be created any other way, he can hire a skilled artist to draw the scene and then film it. Obviously, the use of this technique is limited because few audiences will be fooled for very long by an animation that is supposed to be the real thing. But for a few special scenes where everything else fails, animation will fill the bill.

Then there are one-of-a-kind effects that are created for special movies. In *Beginning of the End,* a movie history of the atomic bomb made in 1946, it was necessary to recreate the dropping of an atomic bomb on Hiroshima, but no usable films of that tragic event were available. The special effects men used a cloud of dye in water to reproduce the mushroom cloud of the bomb. In *The Good Earth,* a film about the troubles of a Chinese family, one trouble was a plague of locusts, which was shown without using any insects. Special effects man A. Arnold Gillespie used a water jar filled with swirling coffee grounds to simulate the insects, joining that image with an image of the Chinese peasants trying to fight off the "locusts." When the camera had to show the Wicked Witch of the West skywriting in *The Wizard of Oz*, the special effects department used an incredible mixture—sheep dip in milk—to give the effect of smoke in the sky.

Of course, one way to create an effect is to have it done life-size in the studio. For the scene in *The Wizard of Oz* where Dorothy is carried away by the flying monkeys, the studio first tried to use animation. When that did not look realistic enough, the special effects men used men dressed as monkeys and hung them from wires—wires that had to be carefully painted and lighted so the camera would not detect them.

And when John Ford filmed a South Seas film titled *The Hurricane*, in 1937, the climactic scene used a full-sized native village (built on the studio lot), with a beach and a lagoon that was actually a water tank. Wind machines—powerful propellers—whipped the water into a froth, while hoses were used to spray the actors and the setting, and underwater pistons churned up waves. The result was a scene that still can draw gasps from audiences when the film is screened.

For the earthquake in the final scene of *San Francisco*, some of the effect was created by having full-sized sets, complete with actors, actually shaking back and forth. And for a more recent scene of similar destruction, the collapse of the freeway in *Earthquake* was done on a road that never moved an inch. Instead, it was the camera that moved, rocking back and forth in a way that looks (on film, at least) as if the freeway is quivering under the shocks of the earthquake. By undercranking the camera—running the film through slower than normal—the final effect showed automobiles that seemed to be speeding hopelessly out of control. (And for a one-of-a-kind shot, the scene of the office tower bending under the stress of the quake was filmed by using a flexible plastic mirror. The mirror was bent to create the illusion of the crumbling of the tower, which actually remained intact.)

With all of these works of ingenuity, much of the work of the special effects department would be impossible without models—or miniatures, as the experts prefer to call them, to distinguish between dime-store models and the incredibly accurate reproductions produced for the probing eye of the movie camera. Quite often, these miniatures are used interchangeably in scenes with full-sized sets, and they are so realistic that audiences never can tell the difference. In the earthquake of *San Francisco* and the quake of *Earthquake*, the special effects experts cut quickly from full-sized shots of sets and actors to shots of miniatures with no apparent transition. And when matte shots are used in co-ordination with realistic sets and miniatures, even the most trained eye can be fooled by the results.

Miniatures take real timing with the camera, which has to be synchronized in scale with the scene being filmed: The smaller the scene, the faster the camera must run to produce a realistic result. The avalanche scene in *Seven Brides for Seven Brothers*, one of the crucial shots in the movie, was actually minuscule in size; by running the film many times faster than the usual twenty-four frames per second, the illusion of a mountain of snow crashing down was created. In *Tora, Tora, Tora*, a stunningly realistic recreation of the Japanese attack on Pearl Harbor, the cameras were run at fifteen times the normal speed to make the miniature explosions come out right on film. (Just to show how the distinction between a miniature and a set can be blurred, one of the ships that was reproduced for the movie was a full-sized replica of a Japanese battleship, which looked peculiar to on-the-scene spectators but perfect to movie audiences.)

Models were very much in evidence when the disaster-film boom hit Hollywood in the 1970s. *The Towering Inferno*'s skyscraper would not have been possible without expert work by the miniature-makers, and many of the scenes from *Earthquake* relied on miniatures. For example, when a truck loaded with cattle rocketed off the freeway, a real truck was used until the last instant, when a miniature was substituted. The special effects department made sure that the transition was invisible to the eyes of the audience.

"Miniature" is a relative term, because many of the models built for Hollywood epics are anything but small. When Victor Mature, playing Samson, pulled down the temple in Cecil B. DeMille's *Samson and Delilah*, the model of the temple was nearly forty feet high, and the model of the idol's statue in the temple was nearly twenty feet high. The scene of the temple's destruction took nearly a year to prepare and cost more than $100,000 to film, using both real people, who were put into the scene by a matte shot, and miniatures of people built to the scale of the temple model.

Some models are elaborate almost beyond belief. For the first version of *Ben Hur*, made in 1926, special effects men built not only a full-sized set of the Circus Maximus of ancient Rome but also a model that could be used to reduce the need for extras. The model included galleries with thousands of "spectators" who could be made to leap to their feet and wave their arms mechanically. And for *Earthquake*, an eighty-foot-high model of the upper six stories of a Los Angeles office building was con-

The climactic scene from Cecil B. DeMille's Samson and Delilah, *showing special effects at their best. (Paramount, 1949)*

structed for the purpose of being wrecked during the quake.

No single one of these techniques is good enough to fill all the requirements for an epic film. One of the major jobs of the special effects department is to fit trick camera shots, miniatures, special sets, and stunts together so realistically that theater audiences will accept the blend without hesitation. In *Earthquake*, to give one example of such blending, matte shots of destruction were combined with life-sized shots of plastic "debris" dropping on or near actors, and a real hunk of concrete weighing nearly seven tons was actually dropped on a car, because no other way of crushing the car realistically was available to the moviemakers.

With all these elaborate effects, some of the most impressive scenes in epic movies are achieved by simple and relatively inexpensive means. The scene showing downtown Los Angeles devastated by the quake in *Earthquake* is actually a still photo, combined with skillful painting, with only the smoke and flames (coming from behind the sheeting on which the photo was processed) being real. And when King Vidor, directing *War and Peace,* ran out of money but still had to film a scene showing a packed opera house, he used a color photo of a crowd in La Scala, the Milan opera house, added some pieces of tinfoil that would wave in the breeze from an electric fan to simulate opera viewers fanning themselves—and got a scene so effective that no one could guess it had been done for almost no money at all.

Fire and Water

FIRE HAS ALWAYS HELD A FASCINATION for most people, a fascination that probably dates back to the origins of the human race, when the flickering campfire was the center of all human activity. And so fire is one of the sure-fire special effects that epic makers can produce to keep an audience enthralled—as witness the instant success of *The Towering Inferno*.

Playing with fire isn't easy, and there are stunt men and women who make a specialty of one of the most dangerous shots that anyone can film: the scene of a man or woman, apparently on fire, rolling in agony as the flames consume living flesh. The secret of this shot is a special suit made of two or three layers of asbestos underwear, and covered with a padded jump suit. The stunt person who does the fire scene must be sealed in completely, which means that he must rely on a hidden breathing apparatus containing no more than three minutes of oxygen. To do the scene, the costume is smeared with alcohol and benzene, maybe with rubber cement added to give some nice greasy smoke, and then is ignited. Within less than three minutes of ignition, the scene must be filmed and the stunt man must be unzipped from the suit to prevent suffocation or damage from heat, which makes itself felt even through all the protective layers.

Compared to such hazardous efforts, the job of showing a burning city on film is relatively easy. One way is to build a full-sized set and then set fire to it—a method that was adopted for the epic scene showing the burning of Atlanta in *Gone With the Wind*. Needless to say, the director who chooses this method has to be confident that everything will go right the first time, because there can be no second chance, and so a more usual method is to use models.

Although they seem to be consumed by flames, models can be burned over and over again, with a slight touch-up of paint and a few repairs if the precise effect that is desired is not achieved the first time. To show Nero fiddling—actually playing the lyre—while Rome burned in *Quo Vadis?*, the special effects men built a plaster model of Rome that covered some nine hundred square feet, with gas fed in to keep the flames going. Hoses and fire extinguishers could put out the fires quickly so that the set would suffer minimum damage if another take was needed. Or if a full-sized set is used, a grand fire effect can be created without burning everything down by using a film version of flame-throwers to put fire where it will be most visible and least destructive. And, of course, all these techniques can be used together, combined by the skill of the special effects man—miniatures, flame guns, life-sized sets, and stunt men in special fire suits to give the audience the thrill that the epic promises.

One special kind of fire effect uses explosives, which are an essential element of any war epic, and which are more carefully controlled than any other kind of special effects. To be a duly qualified explosives expert, an applicant must first have two and a half years of experience as a prop handler, then have fifteen hundred hours handling ordinary special effects, then pass an explosives course approved both by the state of California and the Federal Bureau of Investigation and then pass a security check, necessary to make sure that explosives are not being placed in the wrong hands. Even then, the applicant is merely a Class Three powderman, just a beginner at the trade.

The need for movie realism is one reason for such care. Take *The Bridge on the River Kwai*, the 1957 antiwar epic whose climactic scene was the blowing up of the bridge just as a trainload of troops began to cross it. One mistake in staging that explosion would have cost a great deal of money and time. But more important than money or time is human life, and most of the explosives set off for the movies are ignited with actors nearby—again, no place for amateurs.

This careful attitude toward explosives contrasts with the rather lighthearted approach of the movies' early days, which was evident in an episode involving the comedian Harold Lloyd. He was posing for a publicity photo one day next to a tableful of fake bombs when the photographer asked Lloyd to light his cigarette from the fuse of a fake. Lloyd lit the fuse—and the result was a powerful explosion that caused serious damage not only to him but also to the room. It seems that a real bomb, loaded with flash powder, had gotten mixed in with the fakes by mistake.

No one gets blown up in Hollywood these days, despite numerous scenes in which soldiers and other service-men are surrounded by explosions on land, sea, and in the air. On the ground, the usual method of keeping such war scenes safe is essentially the same as that developed by special effects man Harry Redmond for the World War I movie, *What Price Glory,* which was made in 1926. The explosives are placed in conical metal pots and are topped with peat moss, cork, or other material that will provide a lifelike cloud of dust. The cone focuses the force of the blast upward, and the explosive is set off by electrical impulses flashed through a wire, thus getting the right timing to insure safety.

A well-trained stunt man and some special equipment can provide an even more realistic shot of a soldier ap-parently being blown up by an explosion. As the blast goes off (and it need not be a large one, since even a small amount of explosives can create an impressive cloud), the stunt man will hit a trampoline and rocket into the air, apparently blasted to bits but really landing safely.

To create the impression of an actor being shot, the special effects department will use a small explosion on the actor himself. First, a metal plate will be placed over the part of the body where the "bullet" is supposed to hit. A small explosive cap is placed on the plate and, for more realism, a sac of stage "blood" goes over the cap, which is set off electrically. For the final scene in *Bonnie and Clyde,* in which Faye Dunaway, playing Bonnie, was shot to death, scores of these caps were used, being set off in precise sequence to make it appear as if a machine gun was stitching bullets across her body. To add to the gruesome realism of the scene, it was filmed in slow mo-tion. Bullet holes in the car were produced by punching

holes in the car body, putting in explosive caps and filling
in the holes, then setting off the caps.

Breaking glass is another specialty. For shots that shatter automobile windshields, a small pellet filled with pe-
troleum jelly is shot into the glass, spattering to create
the proper impression. And it used to be a sweet experience for a character to go through a window, because the
window was made of transparent sugar. But since sugar
windows tend to melt under the hot studio lights, sheet
glass now is imitated by special plastics that will shatter
in the same way as glass but without the sharp, pene-
trating points that could be a menace to the stunt man or
actor.

Explosions at sea, a staple ingredient of any naval epic,
require equal amounts of skill. The basic ingredients are
a miniature ship, an explosive charge scaled to the size of
the miniature, and a camera that is run fast enough to
capture a realistic impression from that fleeting explosion.
In *Tora, Tora, Tora,* probably the most impressive naval-
war epic in terms of special effects, the American ships
were one-sixteenth normal size—about forty feet long—
and yet the explosions can hardly be told from the real
thing.

Water is always a problem in such miniature explosions, because water in miniature doesn't blow up in the
same way as real-life amounts of water. In *Tora, Tora,
Tora,* gypsum was added to the water to produce the
proper effect—just one example of how special effects
men have mastered the art of miniaturization.

Their mastery is such that just about any scene of ships
at sea will be a shot of a miniature in a studio tank. Times
have changed since the first *Ben Hur,* when full-sized
vessels were used for the battle at sea. In the 1959

A scene of carefully planned havoc from the war epic Tora, Tora, Tora. (*Twentieth Century-Fox, 1970*)

remake of *Ben Hur,* the same scene was done using mini-atures, saving not only money but also eliminating the risk to extras and actors of being on a sinking ship.

It is surprising how well the special effects department can reproduce a roaring sea in a studio tank only a few hundred feet square and a few feet deep. Detergent is added to produce the foam of a storm at sea; often, blue dye is used to hide the cables needed to pull the minia-ture ships. Huge fans whip the water up to the desired turbulence. Such is the skill of the special effects depart-ment that the results are almost always better than the real thing, as some moviemakers have found out in recent years.

For the sea epic, *The Caine Mutiny,* director Edward Dmytryk gave up trying to film an amphibious assault scene because rough seas made the actors hopelessly seasick. And while no such problems interfered with the full-sized royal barge built for the Elizabeth Taylor *Cleopatra,* the cost of that ship added to the troubled epic's monumental financial difficulties.

Of course, when the scene requires lots of water, lots of water can be supplied on demand. There are two basic tools of the trade: dump tanks, which, as their name implies, will release thousands of gallons of water instantly; and water cannons, which heighten an effect by shooting streams of water at any target.

No one who saw *The Towering Inferno* will forget the cascade of water in the final scene that extinguished the blaze—a cascade created by using miniatures and dump tanks. And in *The Poseidon Adventure,* the scene in which the ship capsizes required not only dump tanks but also six high-powered water cannons, as well as a corps of trained stunt men and women and a set more than one hundred feet long that could tilt up to thirty degrees. That set was built so that it could also be used upside down, as required in the plot.

None of this is as easy as it sounds, and there is always danger when such effects are not handled by experts. But safety regulations now have greatly reduced the chances of accidents happening.

Sometimes a combination of full-sized ships and studio effects will be used, as in the case of the 1962 remake of *Mutiny on the Bounty.* Not only did the studio build a seagoing vessel that was one-quarter bigger than the original *Bounty,* but a full-sized "miniature" was also built on an MGM sound stage, equipped with dump tanks that

The 1962 version of Mutiny on the Bounty, *showing one of the three ships that was built for the movie. This seagoing vessel was actually larger than the original Bounty.* (*MGM, 1962*)

permitted the director to create any sort of storm the script called for. Yet another full-sized model was constructed for scenes in port, and a fourth cutaway version of the *Bounty* was built for filming the below-deck scenes. All the studio models were on rockers to make storm effects more realistic.

And then all the critics said that the first version of *Mutiny on the Bounty,* done in black and white and on a much smaller version, was better. Money can't buy happiness, even in Hollywood.

Up in the Air

AVIATION AND THE MOVIES WERE BORN at just about the same time, and there has been a continuing love affair between the two industries ever since. When the movies were young, flying was not the routine, everyday means of transportation that it is today. It was a romantic field of adventure, populated by daredevils who would risk their lives to set a distance record or do an impossible stunt. Hollywood capitalized on that romance in a long series of aviation epics, which were made not only because the public was entranced by the subject but also because the moviemakers themselves, being showmen, were equally fascinated by flying and fliers.

The heyday of the "barnstormer," wandering aviators who flew their rickety aircraft from town to town to put on impromptu shows and earn whatever they could, was in the 1920s. World War I had ended, leaving behind not only a lot of surplus biplanes but also a lot of surplus aviators, who had been trained for combat but who now found themselves grounded. They would fly into a small town, set up shop in a pasture or county fair, taking people up for rides at bargain rates or performing acrobatics, mock dogfights, wing-walking, parachute jumps, or any other stunt that anyone would pay to see.

Inevitably, smart barnstormers gravitated toward Hollywood, where the money was good and the publicity was better. Before long, movies were full of such stunts as a man transferring from airplane to airplane in midair, a flier jumping from a train to an airplane or vice versa, airplanes flying under bridges or airplanes crashing into the ground, into houses, or into anything else that was available.

In the early days there was very little faking and very few safety precautions. If the scene called for an airplane crash, a flier crashed his airplane into the ground. That stunt was possible only because it had been discovered that by letting one wing of the airplane hit the ground first, the wing absorbed most of the impact, giving an excellent chance of survival for the aviator. But with safety measures on such a primitive level, accidents were inevitable and the toll of death and injuries was terribly high —so much so that the survivors swaggeringly called themselves a "squadron of death."

But the moviemakers got what they wanted—aerial footage so impressive that it still is talked about. Perhaps the greatest of the early aviation epics was *Wings*, a World War I flying story that won the Academy Award in 1928. It was directed by William A. Wellman, himself a veteran of wartime flying, who hired not only the best flying stunt men in Hollywood but also some of the Army Air Force's most skillful aviators to film the scenes of aerial fighting.

Some of the stunts needed for *Wings* were unusually difficult, including a scene showing a crash-landing and another showing a fighter crashing to earth just after takeoff. And the aircraft used in those stunts needed a lot of work, because they had deteriorated badly in the years since the war. But the scenes were done with such skill and care that there were no deaths—although one stunt man suffered a broken back filming one scene. (True to the daredevil nature of his profession, he climbed out of his hospital window and went dancing a few weeks later, to the distress of his doctors.)

It was a different story with the next epic, *Hell's Angels*, which was produced and directed by Howard Hughes, then a young millionaire (the billions were yet to come) who decided to make movies with the profits of his other enterprises. *Hell's Angels* was far more expensive than Hughes had planned. One reason was the arrival of sound in Hollywood in the midst of shooting. With silent films suddenly out of style, many scenes that had already been filmed for the silents had to be scrapped and redone in sound. But Hughes's insistence on the utmost realism also increased expenses, not only in money but also in lives.

Before shooting began, Hughes invested more than half a million dollars in buying and renovating wartime airplanes. For the scenes of dogfights and other aerial stunts, Hughes insisted on doing dozens of takes, urging the fliers on to increasingly daring efforts. At one point, two stunt pilots who were enacting a dogfight became so carried away that they actually began trying to bring each other down, not with bullets but by brushing the aircraft out of control. Such indifference to safety had an inevitable result. One pilot died when his plane hit telephone wires on a ferrying flight from one airfield to another. A mechanic died in a

Wings, *perhaps the greatest of the early aviation epics.*
(*Paramount, 1927*)

crash scene; he was sitting in the back of the airplane controlling smoke pots and crashed with the plane when the pilot bailed out—an incident that drove that pilot out of the movies. Another flier died in a forced landing.

Then came an even worse incident, during the filming of an aviation film titled *Such Men Are Dangerous* in 1930. Three aircraft flew out over the Pacific to film a scene, and two of them collided, killing ten members of the film crew. Public disgust and industry fears about further incidents effectively ended the daredevil era of flying films after that crash. In the next aviation epic, *Dawn Patrol,* actor Richard Barthelmess did his aerial scenes in an aircraft that was hung by cables just twenty-five feet above the ground; farther than that he wouldn't go. From then on, Hollywood created its flying thrills through the use of miniatures, not by using the real thing. The focus shifted from the daredevil flier to the craftsman who meticulously produced miniatures good enough to fool the probing eye of the camera. And it turned out that special effects men could produce on the ground just about any scene that had once required real airplanes and the risk of death.

Almost, but not quite. For *Air Mail,* a 1932 John Ford epic about the early days of commercial aviation, almost all the flying scenes were done on specially designed sets, built to recreate not only realistic miniatures of aircraft but also mountain landscapes that could not be told from the real thing. By constructing special tracks and cranes to move cameras and models of such things as airplane cockpits, the special effects men got results that fooled even the most searching eye. The basic principle of using miniatures—aircraft perhaps fifty times smaller than the real ones—was to run the camera proportionally faster, which eliminated almost all of the telltale indicators that a model was being used. Whatever could not be done with miniature scenery could be done with process shots, using back projection of skies and mountains.

But when it came to a scene in which a daredevil flier flew his airplane through an open hangar, no fakes would do. Daring as they were, the established stunt fliers in Hollywood unanimously refused to attempt that feat. The challenge was accepted by a new man, Paul Mantz, whose success at this and other equally daring stunts made him one of the movie industry's leading stunt fliers.

Unless it could be avoided, though, directors preferred to keep their aviation epics firmly on the ground, even when that required a lot of painstaking effort to co-ordinate miniatures and full-sized sets. For *Test Pilot,* a 1938 film starring Spencer Tracy and Clark Gable as daredevil fliers of experimental airplanes, one key scene showed the crash of a four-engine bomber. The actual crash was done with a miniature, but the studio also built a full-sized set that meticulously reproduced the crashed airplane. Since the full-sized set was built first, the special effects men had to rehearse with five cameras for three days before they were certain that their tiny crash would duplicate the life-sized crash scene on the set.

It was World War II that brought the aviation epic to a new peak. With audiences flocking to see movies about the war in the air, the studios created the necessary scenes with a combination of real footage shot by combat cameras, miniature-scenes, studio sets, and stunt men. Sometimes the miniatures grew to truly impressive size. In *Air Force,* a 1943 Howard Hawks epic that showed the adventures of a single bomber in the days after Pearl Harbor, most of the amazing realistic scenes of warfare, ranging from Wake Island to Bataan and back, made ample use of miniatures. For the climactic scene, showing the destruction of a Japanese fleet by American bombers, the miniatures of the Japanese ships were twenty-five feet long, too big for the studio tanks; the scenes had to be made in the Pacific off Southern California. And even those were dwarfed by the most impressive war aviation movie of them all, *Tora, Tora, Tora,* made years after the actual fighting had ended.

Despite all these years, the aviation epic is still a Hollywood staple, as the success of *Tora, Tora, Tora* shows. There have been epics about the war (such as *Twelve O'Clock High,* in which Paul Mantz got an unprecedented $6,000 for a single scene in which he crash-landed a real B-17) and peacetime epics such as *Airport,* for which Universal built a full-sized model of an airliner, which is still on view for those who take the studio's guided tours. Indeed, it could be said that the brief cycle of epics about outer space, such as *Destination Moon, Marooned,* and *2001: A Space Odyssey,* merely continued the long story of the public's (and the studio's) fascination with flying. For these efforts, of course, the special effects man did almost everything, since outer space can't be filmed in any other way.

But the wheel came full circle when George Roy Hill directed *The Great Waldo Pepper,* the 1975 film about the 1920s barnstormers that starred Robert Redford. Hill, himself an experienced flier, insisted on everything being filmed in the air, with no process shots, something that had not been attempted since *Wings.* To the horror of the studio's stockholders, Hill even talked Redford into climbing out on the wing of a biplane at an altitude of three thousand feet. The final scene, in which Redford

The aviation epic revisited: a wing-to-wing human trans-fer in The Great Waldo Pepper. (*Universal, 1975*)

(playing Waldo Pepper) and Bo Brudin (playing a World War I German ace, Ernst Kessler) fight a movie air battle that turns into a real dogfight, was filmed in the air with Hill at the camera. The aviation epic is still thriving, and so is the daredevil flier. Indeed, the stunt man and woman, on the ground and in the air, remain essential ingredients of any movie epic.

Crashes, Wrecks, Duels, Dives, Falls, and Flips

THE HOLLYWOOD STUNT BUSINESS WASN'T PLANNED; it just happened. In the earliest days of the movies, there was no such thing as a stunt man. Actors were expected to do their own stunts. Indeed, the success or failure of comedians in the studio of Mack Sennett was largely determined by their ability to take the physical punishment and do the flips and falls demanded by that master of physical comedy.

Supposedly, the first stunt men got started when Hollywood epics began to demand feats that most actors would rather not attempt. It was an informal beginning. In those days, extras got about five dollars a day (with the exception of "dress extras," who were given an extra couple of dollars for providing their own dress clothing for fancy scenes). When a film called for a scene such as a fall off the walls of Babylon for *Intolerance,* it was only natural for the director to turn to the assembled crowd of extras and ask if anyone wanted to earn another five dol-

The chariot scene in the modern version of Ben Hur.
Despite accidents, the scene was filmed without loss of life.
(*MGM, 1959*)

lars by staging the stunt. The protection was minimal—no more than a bale of hay or the like to cushion the fall—but there was sure to be one extra who needed money enough to try. Those who didn't have the physical ability or the intelligence to avoid injury were soon weeded out, and a corps of stunt people was born.

Some stars did make a point of doing their own stunts. Comedians Buster Keaton and Harold Lloyd were widely publicized for rarely using doubles, and Douglas Fairbanks, a muscular star of silent films, was celebrated for performing in all the swordfights, jumps, duels, and the like with which his movies were filled. But the inevitable wear and tear of years of moviemaking eventually told on these rugged individuals; even Fairbanks, in his later years, quietly began using doubles for some of his more spectacular stunts.

Make no mistake about it, stunting has always been a dangerous business. Hollywood history is full of tragic injuries and deaths that accompanied the filming of spectacular scenes. In the early days, the major part of the risk came from a lighthearted approach to danger, an approach that kept safety measures to a minimum. But even today, lives are lost in spite of every precaution.

Some movies have become notorious because of the toll they took in lives, both human and animal. The first version of *Ben Hur* is said to have cost the lives of more than a hundred horses in the filming of the chariot race. There were twelve four-horse chariots in the sequence, ten of them driven by stunt men and two driven by the film's stars, Ramon Novarro and Francis X. Bushman. To get the utmost in realism, the drivers were encouraged to run a real race, with bonuses promised to the winners.

Both horses and men were run to their limit, with many of the animals having to be destroyed.

The scandal created by such ruthless methods was so long-lasting that even more than thirty years later, the makers of the second version of *Ben Hur* were plagued by rumors that a similar slaughter had taken place— rumors that were given impetus when Andrew Marton, the head of the second unit that filmed the race sequence, made a bitter remark at a press conference about "twenty men and a hundred horses" being killed in the film. Although Marton was only being ironic, some reporters at the press conference took him seriously.

In fact, although the race was hard on both men and horses, there were no reported deaths and a minimum of injuries, considering the dangerous nature of the sequence. About the only thing that the two versions of the chariot race had in common was the curious fact that the most effective scene in both was the result of an accident. In the 1924 version, a wheel of one of the chariots flew off, causing an unplanned crash that wrecked four chariots and killed five horses. The wreck was captured on film and provided some breathtaking footage for the movie. In the 1958 film, a scene in which a chariot went over a ramp, faking a jump over a wrecked chariot, nearly ended in disaster when the horses hit the ramp too fast, throwing the stunt man driver out of the chariot. By some miracle, the stunt man was not injured seriously. The footage was used in the film for a sequence in which Charlton Heston is supposedly thrown from his chariot and dragged behind, then crawls back on to win the race.

The reason why Hollywood now tries to avoid killing horses is not through warmhearted sentiment but because

The charge from The Charge of the Light Brigade, *a scene that took a great toll of men and horses.* (*Warner Brothers, 1936*)

of legal action that was taken by a number of humane groups who were appalled by the carnage involved in making many films of the 1930s. Perhaps the most notorious of those films was *The Charge of the Light Brigade,* the 1936 epic starring Errol Flynn. The charge that climaxed the picture (and which took longer to show on the screen than it did to occur in real life) was made in a rocky valley in northern California, using an army of stunt men and an endless supply of horses. Because trenches and pits had to be dug to film the scene, the valley became an obstacle course, with men injured and horses killed daily.

The methods used for horse scenes in those days were brutally effective. For scenes in which a horse had to go over a cliff, a filmmaker would do exactly that—send a horse over a cliff, usually to its death. To film a horse falling, the standard method was a rig called a "running W," which used a cable to pull the horse's legs out from under. Although supporters of the method say it is harmless if used properly—among other precautions, the fall should take place in a specially prepared, soft, sandy spot —overuse of the running W by careless filmmakers has brought it into bad repute. Today, falls are made by using trained horses, who have been taught how to take a realistic tumble on a signal from the rider. The riders themselves have mastered methods of taking a fall without being injured—methods that you can see any Sunday on television when you see professional football players bounce up like rubber balls after collisions that would be bone-breaking to an untrained amateur.

While horses are usually the main animal ingredient of epics, many other species show up to make such films more spectacular. The animal trainer is sort of a specialized stunt man, being skilled in providing properly tamed individuals of any species the director may desire. Cecil B. DeMille always liked to have a leopard or a lion wandering around his epic scenes, while gorillas have provided the menace in more movies than can be mentioned. Your screen "gorilla" almost invariably is a man wearing a hairy costume, but lions, leopards, and other beasts are usually present in person, which often makes the stars of such scenes rather uncomfortable. There is a story about Victor Mature, who was supposed to fight a real lion for the DeMille epic *Samson and Delilah,* refusing outright despite reassurances that the lion was tame. "But Victor," the director said, "there's nothing to worry about. He was raised on milk."

"So was I," the actor replied. "But I eat meat now." The scene was done with a stand-in.

And just for the record, the most fabulous movie animal of all, the star of *King Kong,* never really existed. Most of the film was shot using eighteen-inch models of the giant ape in miniature backgrounds and process shots. A twenty-foot-high version of Kong's head and shoulders was built, as was a full-scale mechanical hand for the scenes in which Kong carried off the heroine, Fay Wray, but that was the closest that Kong came to an actual existence. Although an infinite amount of time and effort was needed to make *King Kong* by this method, the results were worth it. For proof, just compare *King Kong* in the original with the endless series of Japanese remakes. Japanese filmmakers use men wearing gorilla suits on miniature sets for their monster movies, with results that are noticeably inferior to the more expensive model technique.

In addition to animal scenes, another tried-and-true in-

A stunt man takes a tumble during the exciting chase in John Ford's Stagecoach. (*United Artists, 1939*)

gredient of Hollywood epics is the automobile scene— race or crash—which has reached new heights of daring in recent years as audiences demand more and more thrills. Probably the most spectacular auto scene in the movies came from real life—an aerial shot of the Indianapolis 500 of 1968 made for the Paul Newman film *Winning*, in which he plays a race driver. Movie cameras brought in to capture typical racing scenes caught the most untypical moment in 500 history—an accident that wrecked three-quarters of the cars in the starting field just seconds after the race began.

Hollywood's special effects men and stunt men could never match that scene of real destruction, but they do their best. Over the years, techniques have been perfected for sending cars over cliffs to particularly striking scenes of demolition, with pieces of the car coming off in precisely timed sequence and the whole wreck ending with spectacularly pleasing balls of flame and smoke. For *Grand Prix*, a 1966 racing epic, director John Frankenheimer had his special effects crew build an air-powered cannon that could fire a full-sized racing car off into space at speeds up to one hundred miles per hour. To get an ultrarealistic view of a crash, Frankenheimer mounted a camera in one such car at eye level as the car rocketed into the ocean, using the footage to put the audience almost literally in the driver's seat.

(Just to show that such all-out efforts might not be needed to achieve realistic effects, consider the airplane crash scene from Alfred Hitchcock's thriller, *Foreign Correspondent*. Hitchcock wanted to show a pilot's eye view of an airliner crashing into the sea. He did it by building a set showing the pilot's compartment, then putting a screen made of thin paper in front of it. Footage showing the water getting nearer and nearer was rear-projected on the paper screen. At just the right moment, water cannon fired bursts through the screen, destroying the paper so quickly that the viewing audience never noticed. The rest of the sequence, showing the stars struggling in the ocean, was filmed in the studio tank.)

While the real crash scene from *Winning* could not possibly be topped, the auto chase from *Bullitt,* the 1968 detective story, is probably the best special effects auto sequence involving stunt men—in this case drivers, who could handle the unusually tricky effort of steering cars over and around the hills of San Francisco. Lest you think that the scene could take place in real life, you should know that the automobiles in the sequence had to be specially strengthened to take the searing turns, leaps, and spins shown on the screen. Of course, the chase ends with the villains' car going up in a smashingly spectacular burst of flame. Just for comparison, the San Francisco chase sequence in the Peter Bogdanovich comedy, *What's Up Doc?,* which ended with cars catapulting into the bay and which was done for laughs, required an equal amount of skill. The cars in the chase had to demolish a sheet of plate glass, tangle with a Chinese New Year's parade, mess up the life of a sign painter on a tall ladder, and weave in and out in tight formation, which called on all the ability of the stunt drivers. And just think about the driving skills needed to film the incredible sequence in *The French Connection,* in which an automobile chases an elevated subway train, smashing off pillars, dodging to avoid pedestrians, careening into obstacles until the car finally is reduced to a near-total wreck.

Driving takes skill, which is just one element of the

stunt person's stock in trade. Another requirement is sheer courage, because the element of physical danger is never absent, no matter how routine a stunt is. The usual protection for a stunt man or woman who takes one of those familiar high falls is a stack of collapsible boxes that will absorb the crunch of the fall, but one can never tell what will happen. In the days when Harold Lloyd was filming daredevil comedies high on building ledges, his standard protection was a pile of mattresses. One day, just to see what would happen, someone dropped a dummy on the mattresses; it bounced high in the air and then plummeted into space. Lloyd did the scene anyway.

Air-filled bags are another way of cushioning falls. But there is still that psychological barrier to be overcome in taking a tall fall, no matter how foolproof the protection is. In *Earthquake,* one scene called for about thirty extras to come dashing down the stairs of a skyscraper and to go hurtling into space because the staircase had been severed by the quake. The scene was filmed on a special set, with a bank of airbags below the extras. But the shot had to be done over several times, because the extras unconsciously would hold up at the last minute before going off the end of the staircase—a natural human reaction to the terror of simply running into open space, a fear that the director had to overcome before the scene was done to his satisfaction.

Fear is natural, because people do get hurt. In *Earthquake,* the final scene in which the reservoir dam breaks, inundating Los Angeles, was shot using an elaborate $70,000 model that held some 53,000 gallons of water. But even though the flood was done in miniature, the scenes showing the city's resident's being swept away by the surging waters had to use real people—and one extra fractured his skull (fortunately not fatally) when a jet from a water cannon threw him against a concrete abutment.

The unhappy truth is that stunt men who stay with their profession too long are not good insurance risks. Most stunt men get out of the hazardous business before it is too late; often they become supervisors of stunts, or directors of second units. But the lure of "just one more" is fatal to some. Paul Mantz died in making *The Flight of the Phoenix,* a 1965 film which centers on the idea of a group of survivors of an airplane crash building a new plane from the wreckage to fly to safety. Mantz flew the old airplane for the film, and died when it crashed. He was remembered in a way that is highly unusual for Hollywood: the film was dedicated to him, with a special mention of that fact in the movie's credits. Many stunt men have died doing movies, but none have been remembered in that way.

The cruel fact is that moviemakers prefer to ignore the existence of stunt men, because of the fear that acknowledging their existence might ruin the illusions that Hollywood works so hard to create. Curiously enough, the only major movie where a stunt man plays an important role was the musical, *Singin' in the Rain,* which shows Gene Kelly working his way up from an anything-goes stunt job (crashing airplanes into buildings, riding motorcycles off cliffs) to a first-class Hollywood star—a sequence that never really happened to any real stunt man, incidentally. As long as moviegoers want to believe that their favorite star is risking life and limb to make a swashbuckling epic, Hollywood will not disillusion them.

There are exceptions, of course. Robert Redford did climb out on that airplane wing for *The Great Waldo*

Pepper and Burt Lancaster (who was once a circus acrobat) did many of the stunts for his swashbucklers, *The Crimson Pirate, Flame and the Arrow,* and *Trapeze,* the latter a circus movie that included some of the most realistic trapeze sequences on film. But, alas, most of Hollywood's leading men may be good actors, but they are bad athletes, and that means stunt men are needed to take their falls, make their leaps, and fight their fights.

That was especially true in the grand era of costume epics, when a swashbuckling film was expected to end with a grand duel. Most film stars simply could not handle a sword well enough to fight a realistic duel, which created a wonderful market for stunt men who bore a close enough resemblance to the stars to stand in for them.

One actor, Cornel Wilde, found himself trapped in costume epics because he was an expert fencer, having competed in college. Another, Basil Rathbone, was a skilled fencer who took part in some of the screen's most memorable duels, such as in *Robin Hood* (1938). Errol Flynn and Douglas Fairbanks, Jr., often did their own fighting scenes. But with very few exceptions, the filming of a climactic scene from a swashbuckling spectacular usually meant obtaining a stunt man who resembled the leading man, dressing him appropriately, and then shooting the duel in long camera angles that were arranged strategically to keep the audience from noticing the truth.

While duels remain a standard element in swashbuckling epics, one thing has changed in recent years—the amount of blood shown in such duels. In years gone by, audiences preferred not to see the gore that was shed in swordfights. Today, there seems to be no limit to the amount of blood that audiences will accept, even in

Swashbuckling, modern style: Charlton Heston as Cardinal Richelieu in The Four Musketeers. *(Twentieth Century-Fox, 1975)*

movies that are aimed at the younger segment of the audience. To judge just how great the change has been, it is instructive to compare the 1948 version of *The Three Musketeers,* in which Gene Kelly played the hero, D'Artagnan, with the 1974 version of the same movie (and its related feature, *The Four Musketeers*) directed by Richard Lester and starring Michael York as D'Artagnan.

In both films, the villains fall in platoons beneath the slashing swords of the musketeers. But in the early version, it is all clean-cut fun, with very little blood visible. In the 1974 film, both heroes and villains fight, not only with swords, but also with kicks, shoves, butts, and any other tactic that brings results, however ungentlemanly it might be. And when the villains are skewered in the latest film, the blood spurts like a fountain, as the audience cheers.

The movie "blood" is easily managed. Special effects men have ample supplies of sticky red liquid, including a type that the British cheerfully call "Kensington gore." To show people being skewered, there are a variety of techniques: trick swords in two parts, one for the chest, one for the back, to make it appear that an actor has been run through; knives or arrows that are held flat against the actor's body and that pop upright by spring action; imitation missiles that are fired along invisible wires to impact against a body; dummy bodies or torsos, suitably filled with fake blood, that can be impaled at the director's pleasure to create the right effect.

Whatever the method chosen to depict blood-shedding, fashions have clearly changed since the 1930s, when audiences preferred not to see any sign of blood even though platoons of extras and stunt men were falling victim to arrow, sword, and spear. It was a real shocker when the director of *Gone With the Wind* let the audience get a brief view of the gory results after the heroine shot a wicked soldier up close. Today, such scenes are taken for granted, just one more day's work for the stunt man. You could call it progress.

The Most Expensive Movie Ever Made

THE MOST EXPENSIVE EPIC EVER MADE WAS—an accident.

That's always been true, because movie executives don't like spending money very much. Movie ads may boast about the amount of money lavished on a film, but what the studio heads would really like is to make a movie on a very low budget that looks as if it had cost a lot of money. Almost invariably, the most expensive movies ever made were not designed to be that way. Accidentally, for reasons that couldn't be helped, the director went over his budget, and the studio had no choice but to go along.

Some directors have become notorious because of their penchant for spending money. One of them Erich von Stroheim, who flourished in the wild days of the 1920s, carried that tendency to an extreme. Von Stroheim would shoot hour after hour of film, much more than was needed for any movie—and then keep on shooting for hours and hours more. For one film, *Greed*, Von Stroheim shot forty-two reels of film in 1923 and 1924. That's about seven hours of film. MGM, his studio, cut that down to under two hours for the version that was released, infuriating Von Stroheim. But he outdid himself with a later film, *Queen Kelly*, which was never released. Von Stroheim kept on shooting and shooting, using up film on a story that literally seemed endless, until the studio called a halt. Pieces of *Queen Kelly* have been shown from time to time, but nothing like the movie that Von Stroheim was attempting to make was ever completed.

As for trying to pick an all-time money-spending champion, that contest is complicated by inflation. The value of the dollar has been declining steadily through the twentieth century, so that a million dollars spent on a film in 1914 meant a lot more than the same amount spent on a film in 1974. MGM executives were horrified when director Vincente Minnelli spent an extra half-million dollars on the final ballet scene of *An American in Paris*—perhaps the most acclaimed scene in any American movie musical —in 1951; today, that expense would be accepted with hardly a quibble, because the overall cost of movies has risen stupendously (to use a favorite Hollywood word).

So, in order to pick the candidates for the most expensive movie ever made—the epic of epics, at least as far as sheer dollars expended is concerned—one must take the question an era at a time, putting a movie's budget in context with the standards of that era.

For the teens, the era when both the century and the movies were still young, D. W. Griffith's *Intolerance* deserves special mention. The budget for that film reportedly was in the neighborhood of $2,000,000. But it wasn't just the size of the budget that counted. Griffith's sense of spectacle and fantastic vision made *Intolerance* an epic to remember even today. Maybe someone else spent more money on another early epic, but who remembers anything but *Intolerance* today? (*Birth of a Nation,* an incomparable money-maker, doesn't get a mention because its budget hardly began to compare with *Intolerance.*)

In the 1920s, despite the efforts of Cecil B. DeMille, the money-spending champion probably was the first version of *Ben Hur*—clearly by accident. Zigzagging between Rome and Hollywood, MGM went far over the planned budget. The movie finally cost in the neighborhood of $4,000,000, and that in an era when twenty dollars a week was a decent wage for a working man. That was about five times as much as the studio had planned to spend, and although the film was successful at the box office, it still ended up putting the studio about $1,000,000 in the red.

In the 1930s, there was a clear winner in the epic sweepstakes—a winner that collected not so much on pure reckoning of money spent but on the sheer impact it made not only on the film community but on the nation as a whole. The film was *Gone With the Wind,* and it still has a special place in movie history that no other film can match.

The movie had its start in a best-selling novel written by an Atlanta woman, Margaret Mitchell, about the fate of a single, scheming, beautiful young southern belle, Scarlett O'Hara, during and after the Civil War. Although the novel was astoundingly long—more than a thousand pages, the longest novel published up to that time—it sold at an astounding rate, better than a million copies in its first year. David O. Selznick bought the movie rights for $50,000, an unprecedented figure for that time, and he set out to make a Civil War epic that would sweep the nation off its feet.

There was more than the usual Hollywood braggadocio involved in Selznick's effort, because he was willing to

A scene from Gone With the Wind, *the greatest epic of its day—and maybe of all times.* (Selznick/MGM, 1939)

pay to get the results he wanted. There was one obvious choice to play the role of the leading man, Rhett Butler, a dashing scoundrel, and that choice was Clark Gable, the greatest male star in Hollywood. But Gable was the property of MGM. So, to get the services of Clark Gable, Selznick gave MGM (among other things) distribution rights to *Gone With the Wind,* which turned out to be a long-lasting bonanza for MGM.

The choice of the leading lady was much more difficult. Looking for the perfect Scarlett O'Hara, Selznick screen-tested just about every big star in the movie world. None filled the bill. Dozens of talent scouts were employed to bring in any young, undiscovered actress who might strike screen sparks as Scarlett O'Hara. None of them did. Even after actual filming of the movie started late in 1938, no suitable Scarlett O'Hara had been discovered.

Finally, David Selznick's brother brought in a twenty-five-year-old British actress, Vivien Leigh. She proved to be the perfect Scarlett O'Hara, mastering the necessary southern accent despite her British upbringing. The rest of the cast was also excellent, with such great stars as Leslie Howard and Olivia de Havilland serving opposite Gable and Leigh. In addition, *Gone With the Wind* was made in Technicolor, which now is taken for granted but then was an amazing advance in screen technique. And no expense was spared to make sure that all the scenes, from the happy splendor of the South before the Civil War to impressive scenes of fighting and suffering, were done with realism, sweep, and imagination.

The final cost of *Gone With the Wind* was about $3,200,000, a sum that drew murmurs in those Depression days. For that money, Selznick got one of the longest movies ever made for general release. *Gone With the*

Wind ran three hours and forty minutes, an unheard-of length for an era when the average main feature ran eighty or ninety minutes (kept that short so that the audience could also see a second "B" feature that rounded out the standard double bill).

With the millions of dollars and tons of publicity that had been lavished on *Gone With the Wind,* it was no wonder that everyone connected with the movie—as well as most members of the film community—was praying for success when the movie premiered in Atlanta just before Christmas of 1939. Prayers were answered; *Gone With the Wind* was an instant success, and that success has been confirmed through the years, as the film has been released over and over again, always adding to the profits it has racked up. Other films may have made more dollars than *Gone With the Wind,* but none has had quite the same impact.

To talk dollars, *Gone With the Wind* has taken in more than eighty million of them at the box office. It was more than two decades until a film earned more money than *Gone With the Wind,* and the new champion was a surprise to everyone—*The Sound of Music,* a pleasant but unspectacular musical that turned out to be far more popular than anyone, including its makers, had calculated. The record was broken again in 1972 by *The Godfather,* but by then runaway inflation had cheapened the dollar so much that the comparison was not fair. To those who remember Hollywood as it was, *Gone With the Wind* will reign forever as the box-office king.

As for the film itself, *Gone With the Wind* is a sort of monument to a Hollywood that no longer exists; the Hollywood of huge studios, where the world's greatest movie technicians worked, where armies of young actors and actresses fought to get a place in the top rank of stars, where dreams were made and broken every day, where anything seemed possible and often was. The movie is a long, romantic drama, very well acted and with spectacular scenes, marred by a rosy view of the Confederacy and a view that slavery wasn't really as bad as the history books made out. Whatever it is, *Gone With the Wind* is still great entertainment, with spectacular scenes, such as the burning of Atlanta, alternating with well-acted scenes of drama. It was the kind of movie that audiences of the Depression years wanted, a movie that allowed you to forget your troubles for a few hours as you entered a never-never land created by the magic of Hollywood. As was said earlier, it is a world that has long since vanished, giving way to the grim realism of the 1960s and the 1970s.

No epic dominated the 1940s or the 1950s in the way that *Gone With the Wind* dominated the 1930s. Perhaps a narrow margin should be given to Cecil B. DeMille's second version of *The Ten Commandments,* which was made in 1956 at a cost of $13,500,000 and a running time of three hours and forty-one minutes, just one minute longer than *Gone With the Wind.* If the money sounds impressive compared to the spending of the 1930s, remember inflation; just a few years later, the remake of *Ben Hur* cost $15,000,000 and the second version of *Mutiny on the Bounty* came in at $18,000,000. But none of these films really could match *Gone With the Wind.* With the passage of years and the competition of television, Hollywood had lost something of its old spirit, and the results showed on the screen. All the epics of the 1950s, although they showed clearly that a lot of money had been spent, lacked the vitality of those of the 1930s.

And then came the 1960s, and the movie to end all movies—a movie that very nearly did end a major studio, among the other turmoil it caused. The film was *Cleopatra,* Twentieth Century-Fox's story of the fabulous Serpent of the Nile, which today reigns supreme among epic movies, if only because of the money it cost—a staggering $31,000,000, impressive even in this era of inflation.

It wasn't intended to be that way when producer Walter Wanger began talking with Spyros Skouras, head of Twentieth Century-Fox, about *Cleopatra* in the late 1950s. At that time, the movie was envisioned as just another epic—spectacular, to be sure, but well within the price range of other epics of that time. The original estimate called for a budget of $5,000,000 tops, including the salaries of the stars and a studio in London.

Then things began to happen. After considering a number of possible heroines, including Joanne Woodward and Joan Collins, the choice fell on Elizabeth Taylor. Boy, was it an expensive choice! Miss Taylor began by asking for a cool million dollars. After prolonged negotiations, she accepted a fee reported to be over $1,000,000, plus a percentage of the profits over a set amount. One result of that settlement was to cause a permanent increase in the price of Hollywood stars, who immediately began trying to get fees approaching that paid to Miss Taylor. Another result of the agreement was to send the budget of *Cleopatra* on an upward spiral. No one knew it at the time, but it was a spiral that was to continue for quite a while.

After inspecting the proposed studio at Pinewood in England, Wanger decided that it was too small and didn't look Egyptian. The decision was made to use an Italian studio. That was canceled because of Italian tax laws. Finally a decision: The movie would be made using the studio

The 1963 version of Cleopatra, *the most expensive movie ever made. Elizabeth Taylor and Richard Burton have their backs to the camera. (Twentieth Century-Fox, 1963)*

at Pinewood, but with location shooting in Italy. Workmen began building sets in England, but no one had counted on the British weather, which was terrible. It was decided to shoot the desert shots in the desert, specifically in Egypt. By this time the movie was falling behind schedule and the budget was up to $6,000,000.

The set in England was built—it covered eight acres and used enough building material for a forty-home subdivision. Elizabeth Taylor arrived in England and immediately caught cold, putting her out of action. The filmmakers tried to shoot without her, mustering thousands of extras, but they were stymied by the weather, which continued to be terrible. There was trouble with the script and with the British hairdressers union, whose members went on strike because they objected to Elizabeth Taylor using her own hairdresser, whom she had brought over from the United States. The studio was spending $45,000 a day and between the weather, Elizabeth's cold, and the hairdresser problem, they had very little to show for it.

After more misadventures, including a serious bout of illness that put Elizabeth Taylor in the hospital, and even endangered her life, it was decided to shoot the film in Italy. Everything continued to go wrong. The beach selected for the Alexandria set turned out to be riddled with live mines left over from an invasion in World War II, and the beach next to it was a military firing range, which meant that work had to stop while the guns blasted away. The extras who played *Cleopatra*'s extras and slaves went on strike to protest the skimpy costumes they had to wear. The horses and elephants hired for the big scenes could not get along with each other. By this time, the overhead was up to $67,000 a day, the budget was up to $10,000,000 and shooting had hardly begun.

Preparations began for the grand procession scene, using ten thousand extras who were to be paid ten dollars a day each. It began to rain and kept on raining. Elephants were imported from England. Cats began invading the set to keep warm, and they were followed by dogs; the combination of yowling and barking made shooting impossible, and days were lost as sets were taken apart to root out the cats. The electrical facilities on the set turned out to be inadequate, and more than a hundred American craftsmen were brought to Italy, along with equipment from all over Europe. By this time the budget was over $12,000,000 and climbing.

When Cecil B. DeMille had made *Cleopatra* in the Depression year of 1934, he used a model showing the Egyptian queen's royal barge; mirrors were used to turn a few models into an impressive fleet for the cameras. For the new *Cleopatra,* a full-sized barge was built at a cost of more than $250,000—except that the beach in Italy was too shallow for the barge. A pier had to be built. Then it was discovered that the barge was not powered, which meant that a system of winches had to be built and some tugboats hired to get the barge moving.

In addition to the costs of these errors, there was also the cost of a lavish production. Elizabeth Taylor had more than sixty costumes, including a fifteen-pound, $6,000 ceremonial dress of gold. The two sets built in Italy covered a total of thirty-two acres and cost about $2,000,000. In addition to the royal barge, workmen also built a sphinx sixty-five feet long for Cleopatra's triumphant entry into Rome, and a royal mausoleum, decorated with fifty-six sphinxes, for Cleopatra's suicide scene.

And finally, Elizabeth Taylor and her leading man, Richard Burton, fell in love during the film, which caused an endless number of new complications, since both were

The Soviet version of War and Peace, *certainly one of the most lavish movies ever made, as the number of extras in this scene testifies.* (Mosfilm, 1967)

married to other people at the time. Only that old professional, Rex Harrison, who played Caesar, went through the filming without much turmoil.

The film moved to Egypt for outside shots, partly because the government had promised five thousand soldiers at one dollar a day each. The price was raised to four dollars a day when the unit arrived.

Finally, in 1962, four years after it had begun, *Cleopatra* was finished. The price was more than $31,000,000, far and away the most that had ever been spent on a Hollywood movie. Adding the cost of distribution, promotion, and prints of the film, *Cleopatra* would have to draw more than $40,-000,000 at the box office just to break even. Spyros Skouras was out as head of Twentieth Century-Fox, largely because the studio was in a financial crisis due to the cost of *Cleopatra,* and there was an excellent chance that the studio might fold if the film flopped.

When *Cleopatra* opened in selected theaters across the country, the reviews were mixed. Some critics said that the film was the longest mistake in Hollywood history. The movie ran a staggering four hours and three minutes, and there were many critics who said that was about four hours too long. But many reviewers found plenty to praise about the spectacular production, including the ample signs of the endless money that had been spent to dazzle audiences.

As for the audiences, they came—not in overwhelming numbers, but enough to pull Twentieth Century-Fox back from the brink of bankruptcy. Optimistic predictions by Darryl Zanuck, who had taken over the studio, that *Cleopatra* might gross as much as $100,000,000 proved to be overoptimistic, but the film was not the total failure that some pessimists had anticipated. The money taken in at theater box offices was not enough to put *Cleopatra* into the black, but television finally did the job. In 1968, the American Broadcasting Company agreed to pay $5,000,000 for television rights to *Cleopatra*, showing the film over two evenings. That sum brought the takings of the film to just short of $44,000,000. The most expensive film ever made had turned a profit.

Until now, *Cleopatra* still holds the all-time budget record, even after a decade and more of inflationary cost increases. Hollywood had learned a lesson from the extravagance that went into *Cleopatra*, and executives were keeping a much tighter hold on expenses. With all their crowd scenes and special effects, the great disaster movies of the 1970s, such as *Earthquake* and *The Towering Inferno*, cost only about half as much as *Cleopatra*, and had a much better balance on the profit line. Unless something drastic happens to the value of the dollar in years to come, or unless some studio makes mistakes on the same grand scale as were made during the filming of *Cleopatra*, the 1963 Serpent of the Nile epic seems safe in its unenviable record.

Not that *Cleopatra* stands quite alone. A case could be made for putting the 1968 Soviet production of *War and Peace* on the same level. Directed by Sergei Bondarchuk, this version of Tolstoy's great novel called on a seemingly endless supply of extras and resources, as the Soviet government apparently had decided to spare no expense in recreating this national epic of resistance against the French invasion of 1812. This was one film that truly justified the old Hollywood tag line: "Cast of thousands, years in the making." Its length alone, an unbelievable six hours and thirteen minutes, put the Soviet *War and Peace* in a class by itself. When the film was shown in the United

States, audiences had to come to the theater twice to see the
whole movie, which was shown in two parts. No one will
ever know just how much this *War and Peace* actually cost,
but if the movie had been made in the West, it clearly would
be a rival to *Cleopatra* in the money sweepstakes. Whether
War and Peace showed a profit is something that only the
Soviet government knows. Presumably, no one cares. Mos-
cow isn't Hollywood.

The Epic and the Tube

A TERRIBLE THING HAPPENED TO HOLLYWOOD in the 1950s: television. As the television tube became a standard item in American living rooms (yes, there was a time when television did not exist), Americans began staying home and watching free entertainment rather than going out to pay for movies. Virtually overnight, Hollywood's position at the top of the entertainment industry was undermined, and the movie industry was thrown into the kind of panic it had not experienced since 1928, when the success of *The Jazz Singer* made silent movies obsolete overnight, and studios had to scramble to convert to sound.

The panic of the 1950s was worse, because no one in Hollywood knew what to do to fight the competition of television. But one thing seemed clear: If people could only get a small, black-and-white picture on the TV tube at home, then the movies could do better by offering a big color picture in a theater. As a result, strange things began happening to the size and shape of the movie screen.

For decades, the shape of the movie screen had been standardized at a ratio of four to three—that is, the typical theater screen would be twenty feet wide and fifteen feet high. Suddenly, Hollywood was seized by a fashion for screens that were much wider than the standard, because such screens obviously offered something that television could never hope to match. Movie epics did not become much bigger, but they did become wider.

Widest of all was Cinerama, whose curved screen stretched almost a complete half circle around the audience. The first Cinerama presentation, *This Is Cinerama*, which opened in New York in 1952, had no plot at all, just a series of spectacular scenes. But audiences gasped at the scenes, especially a filmed ride on a roller coaster that just about gave all the thrills of a real ride. More important, the audiences were big ones. Hollywood moguls took a look at the first box-office reports for Cinerama, and the wide-screen scramble in Hollywood was on.

However, the years have not been kind to Cinerama, which never lived up to its original promise. The reasons are largely mechanical: The process requires not only specially prepared theaters, equipped with the wall-to-wall, curved screens, but it also requires three projectors, whose images are carefully matched, to achieve its effects. Since Cinerama features were rather few and far between—it took ten years, until 1962, for Cinerama to produce its first film with a plot, *The Wonderful World of the Brothers Grimm*— most theater owners would not pay the heavy expenses of installing such a system. Today, the original Cinerama system has been virtually abandoned; Cinerama still releases films, but these productions use a single projector and a less expansive screen than the original. The idea does live on in the 360-degree spectacular travelogues that have become popular at world fairs and other expositions. At these presentations, the audience sits in the middle and can look around at a screen that covers a full circle.

Another epic development that seemed revolutionary at the time but also faded away quickly was three-dimensional film. The first three-D film, *Bwana Devil*, also opened in 1952, just a few weeks after the Cinerama premiere. Again, audiences were entranced, even though there were complaints about having to wear special glasses to see the film. The three-D effect is obtained by shooting two slightly overlapping pictures. The special glasses allow one eye to see one picture and the other eye, the other picture; the brain puts the two images together to create the three dimensions. It is the same principle used in the "stereopticons" that once were a fixture in Victorian parlors.

For a brief period it appeared that three-D was the wave of the future, and major studios rushed to make films in the process. But the vogue began to wear off, as the excitement of ducking from spears that were thrown at the audience or of gasping as a lion "leaped" out of the screen quickly faded. Audiences began staying away from three-D movies in droves, and Hollywood stopped making them.

An even quicker burial was afforded a process called "Smell-O-Vision," which was designed to allow the audience to smell as well as view a scene, by the use of special odor projectors. It came and went with a single feature, released in 1960, called *Scent of Mystery*. Hardly a critic was able to resist the obvious line: Smell-O-Vision stank.

With all these false starts, the wide screen did establish itself in the film industry. There were a number of different processes—VistaVision, CinemaScope, Todd-AO, Ultra Panavision (whatever else it has lost, Hollywood has not lost its superspectacular publicity sense)—all of which allowed the audience to see a much wider picture. And along with the wide screen came stereophonic sound, with voices and music coming from more than one loudspeaker. (In 1975, the rock musical *Tommy*, whose sound track was at ear-splitting levels, was carrying on the old Hollywood epic tradition by advertising something called "quintiphonic sound.")

In the 1970s, the wide screen is still here, but it is not the king that it used to be. For one thing, audiences will not come to see a movie just because it is wide; it has to be a good movie as well as being a wide-screen movie. And the wide screen may be great for showing a battle at sea or other spectacular scenes, but it is not so good for showing one actor talking to another actor—there is a lot of leftover screen going to waste in such shots. And even for epics, some directors complain that the wide screen is not tall enough, creating the impression that the movie has been filmed through a mail slot. Today, epics and other films are made in a variety of shapes, from the old standard four-to-three ratio to wide screen.

However wide it may be, today's epic is certain to be long, in terms of minutes. Where Hollywood once advertised the double feature, consisting of a main production and a quickie "B" movie thrown in to fill the evening, today's fashion is for a single blockbuster. The three-hour barrier, first broken by *Gone With the Wind*, has been torn to shreds. *Cleopatra's* four-hour running time has been mentioned; and the films that come close to that include *Lawrence of Arabia, Exodus, The Alamo, Ben Hur, Spartacus*—indeed, an almost endless list. Hollywood may not be making better movies than it did before television, but it is making movies that are longer.

Another lasting change that came with the television era has been the tendency to film epics on location, rather than on studio lots, a trend that has hurt Hollywood employment considerably. Part of the reason is financial. The stars who are getting million-dollar fees for movies have found they can prevent the tax man from getting too much of that money by maintaining residences outside the United States; the producers have followed the stars. In addition, some countries in the years after World War II, when the United States dollar was far stronger than it is now, refused to allow studios to export money their films had earned in those countries; the studios had to use up the money by shooting films in those nations. And as the wages paid to Hollywood extras have been increased by union contracts, the studios wanting to film epic scenes using thousands of extras have gone overseas for cheaper labor.

None of this has made American movie unions very happy, and some stars who have to spit sand out of their mouth or comb insects out of their hair on location, instead of going home to a comfortable Beverly Hills mansion every night, rather regret the change. But the gain in realism for some epics is unmistakable. *The Bridge on the River Kwai* owes some of its most impressive scenes to its shooting location in Ceylon. And *Lawrence of Arabia* would not have been half as spectacular if director David Lean had not been able to capture the eerie atmosphere of the desert on film. To see the wavering figure of a Bedouin riding a camel slowly emerge from the shimmering heat of the desert, or a cavalry charge across the

Lawrence of Arabia, *a movie filmed on location in the desert, with spectacularly realistic results. (Columbia, 1962)*

desert, or bloody battles sweeping across the screen—all this was possible only by taking the camera and the actors to the real scene of action. And *Exodus*, Otto Preminger's three-and-a-half-hour version of the birth of Israel, owed much of what limited effectiveness it had to the fact that it was filmed where the actual incidents took place.

But there was plenty of make-believe in the movies still, because reality often was not good enough for the cameras. Hollywood did go to England to make *Doctor Dolittle*, a no-expenses-barred, wide-screen version of Hugh Lofting's famous children's book, but once there, the film-makers found it necessary to virtually rebuild an English village to make it look picturesque enough for the screen. *Doctor Zhivago*, an epic about the Russian Revolution, was not made in Russia, nor was *55 Days at Peking*, an epic about the Boxer Rebellion, made in China.

But a lot of epics about the Roman Empire were made in Rome, as well as a whole gaggle of costume epics about ancient Greece. Many of them starred Steve Reeves, a former Mister Universe, whose muscles were more impressive than his acting ability. The box-office success of Reeves's film *Hercules* in 1957, partly due to a shrewd advertising campaign, set off what seemed like an endless series of sequels, starring Reeves and other muscle-men. The plots of these Italian costume epics tended to limp along, the films were further marred by the need to dub in the dialogue for American audiences (a job that was often done so ineptly, that the words coming from the sound track and the movement of the actors' lips rarely coincided), and the plastic boulders that the actors threw around were not terribly convincing. But people would pay to see these films, so they were turned out on the assembly line until the fad ended. Later products of the same assembly line, incidentally, were the gory Italian "Spaghetti Westerns" and then the Kung Fu movies, equally gory. Blood and guts definitely were in style in the 1970s.

While all this was happening, the old Hollywood of the golden era began to vanish. The iron grip that the major studios had on the industry loosened and then dissolved, as independent producers took over. There was a visible sign of the change: The back lots where many of Hollywood's greatest epics had been made began to lose their value as sets for movies and to gain a new value as real estate—hundreds of acres of land in the heart of a growing Los Angeles area. Office buildings began to spring up where Babylon and ancient Rome once existed. It was all summed up in the history of MGM, the studio which once advertised that it had "More Stars Than There Are in the Heavens." First, MGM auctioned off the props and costumes from its spectacular days. Then it put up for sale the huge back lot where sets existed for anything from a typical New York street to a medieval castle to a Western town to—anything you could name. Then, in 1974, after years of reverses, MGM stopped making movies. The mightiest studio of them all had fallen.

If there was one constant in all of this change, it was the movie epic. Hollywood may have lost much of its old magic, but it had not lost its ability to produce on the screen sights that were available nowhere else. When the public wanted epics about outer space in the 1960s, Hollywood obliged with such spectaculars as *Marooned* and *2001: A Space Odyssey*, which created mind-boggling views of space without getting a foot off the ground. When the public wanted epics about disasters in the 1970s, Hollywood obliged with *Earthquake* and *The Towering Inferno* and all the rest, creating havoc and destroying cities without bothering anyone but the special effects department. If it was supercomedies that the public wanted, then Hollywood was ready with such products as *It's a Mad Mad Mad Mad World, Those Magnificent Men in Their Flying Machines,* and *The Great Race*—movies that were not really as funny as they were supposed to be, but spilling over with special effects and trying hard to get laughs by being twice as big as life. If the public wanted supermusicals, Hollywood would try. The originality that produced such gems as *An American in Paris* and *Seven Brides for Seven Brothers* was gone, but Hollywood was ready to spend millions on shows bought from Broadway: *Sweet Charity, Funny Lady, The Sound of Music, Tommy*—each spectacular in a different way.

Styles change but the film epic goes on. Once it was togas and chariots, heroes who were square and heroines who were innocent; now it is earthquakes and fire, heroes who are wicked and heroines who are tough. But still, it is the sight that fills the screen and holds the audience rapt, the sight that draws gasps and has people asking, "How did they do that?" which fills the theater. It is the color, the sound, the cast of thousands, the film that has been years in the making which remain Hollywood's sure-fire hit. The miniatures, the wind machines, the huge sets, the armies of extras, the camera techniques are ready when you want them. Just ask—any sight on earth, at any time in history—and the films will provide it. The story of movie epics is just beginning.

INDEX